"*Journaling for Well-Being & Peace* is the essential "how to" book on personal transformation through writing. Elizabeth Welles shows us how to traverse our own lives with fresh eyes that see magic in the mundane, hope in the grief and humor in just about everything. The writing exercises, personal insights and mindfulness practices, taken together, empower us to live our most joyful and reverential lives. It is truly a book of wisdom and love from a wonderfully gifted writer, teacher and actor. Brava!"

> **Lauren Furst**, President of the Unitarian Universalist Congregation at Shelter Rock, and founder of Pathways to Wealth

"What Elizabeth Welles has accomplished with *Journaling for Well-Being & Peace* is astounding. This book is a specific guide to the world of journaling that offers the reader an opportunity to safely explore his or her interior and exterior worlds. Ms. Welles brings a compassionate, unique dimension, depth and breadth unlike any other book about journaling I have seen. Through her own generously shared personal experiences and process, she invites the reader to get a "feel" for their own spirit's Knowing. The beautiful guided meditations are rich with metaphor and opportunity for both deep relaxation and stirring the creative spirit. Her gentle weaving of the body, mind, and soul in her own examples and those of other writers and thinkers, encourages the reader to venture into areas they would not normally go and go to willingly. The people who find this book will be able to dream on paper in ways never before realized, while deepening the peace at their core. Bravo for this fine and impressive work!"

> **Dale Atkins,** Ph.D., Psychologist, author of *Sanity Savers: Tips for Women to Live a Balanced Life*, commentator in the media and frequent guest expert on The TODAY Show

i

"Elizabeth Welles' *Journaling for Well-Being & Peace* is a rich compendium of journaling practices that will take you on a lifelong exploration of your self – as you have been, as you are now, and as you might become in the future. These powerful practices will serve as expert guides as you plumb the depths of your past experiences to retrieve all of their hidden transformational treasures; pause in the present moment to fully appreciate intricate contours of your emotional-motivational body; and playfully create myriad possible future worlds to step into and 'try on'. Whether you're on an established path of self discovery, or wish to carve out your own, this is one book you'll want to have in your satchel."

Peggy La Cerra, Ph.D., Evolutionary Neuroscientist, author of *The Origin of Minds: Evolution, Uniqueness and the New Science of the Self* and featured columnist for *Spirituality and Health Magazine.*

"A seamless blend of writing practices, meditations and personal stories, *Journaling for Well-Being & Peace* will not only nurture your creativity but bring you closer to the intuitive wisdom of your body, mind and soul. A revelatory book!"

Prill Boyle, author of *Defying Gravity: A Celebration of Late-Blooming Women*

Journaling for Well-Being & Peace is a rich resource of practical tools that show you the way back to your own creative wealth, your vision and voice. It is a manual for personal peace that will resonate in your life long after you have finished reading it.

Charlotte S. Hunter, US Director, Pocketful of Joy, Inc.

Elizabeth Welles understands our deepest need to feel connected, heard and understood. In *Journaling for Well-Being & Peace* she offers us paths to wholeness that nurture the psyche and soul.

Susan L. Atchison, founder of A Healing Soul, Ltd.

Journaling
for Well-Being
& Peace

With Stories, Practices, and Meditations

Elizabeth Welles

A PEACE COMMUNICATIONS BOOK

Copyright 2011 by Elizabeth Welles

Published by Peace Communications

Library of Congress Control Number: 2011922313

ISBN: 978-0-9743998-1-2

Printed in the United States of America

Cover Design & Layout by Quoin Design

Copy Edited by Susan Hart Hellman

To two of the brightest lights in my life, my mother, Cathy, who gave me my first book to write in, and my father, Daniel. They have always appreciated, encouraged and supported my love of and life in the arts.

Table of Contents

Acknowledgments

Journaling for Well-Being & Peace began as a short manual in response to a teleseminar I was teaching. The short manual quickly morphed into the book before you. Special thanks go to the women of that teleseminar, and specifically to the women who offered their work to this book. They are Luz Elizabeth Gudino, Lesli Garnett, Katherine Ladd, and Kathleen Purmell. My thanks go out to the many people who came to my journaling classes, and the creativity-spirituality support groups these past twenty plus years.

Deep gratitude goes to my dear friend, Elio Zarmati. Your own work is a source of inspiration, and your constant caring eye to my work is forever appreciated. Thank you for your listening ear on the artist's path, and for just hanging out in Ojai.

Thank you to Susan Hart Hellman for your discerning edit, and for your patience and willingness to jump in for a friend.

Thank you Nance a.k.a. Dana Macy for your cheerleading support of my work.

Thank you to my brother, Rick Shapiro, for your assistance with last minute alterations.

Forever gratitude to my Mother for your constancy and encouragement to always finish the books, and for your beautiful heart, your sweetness and light!

Eternal gratitude and love to the Gracious Spirit Divine of All That Is.

Author's note

In certain places names have been changed to protect the privacy of those mentioned. Beginning chapter quotes, story examples, poems and songs are composed by the author, unless otherwise noted.

Welcome

Journaling for Well-Being & Peace is designed to assist you in your journal process and with meditation-relaxations. It introduces unique foundational journaling practices that are explorative in nature. Diving down the rabbit hole into the wonderful world of words, journaling will help you de-stress and relax. It will enhance your creativity, sharpen your intuition, and deepen your peace. This book covers journaling from healing and catharsis, to creativity, and writing as social action.

The journal is infinite in variety and can include, but is not limited to, the written journal, visual journals, audio journals and video journals, storytelling and story sharing. Journals are used for an infinite number of purposes: dream journals, diet journals, first year of your baby's life journal, political journals, letter journals, holiday and vacation journals, photo journals, and so forth.

Journaling is a form of writing that can be as free-associative as you want it to be or as directive as you want it to be. When working with individuals in groups, a specific topic is sometimes recommended. But more often, topic is left to individual choice, and I simply teach the techniques that can be applied to any number of situations and circumstances.

The seven meditations in this book are an important component for entering into the quiet. In a world with frenetic noise, it is the silence that I relish. It is not a silence of lying down to go to sleep, but one that is vibrantly alive, from where the deepest embers of creativity are stirred. In meditation and relaxation, and in contemplative solitude, a deeper awareness of one's own Self can be seen, witnessed and heard. It is a silence and stillness born of strength and verve that has the ability to lift up one's Self and therefore the world.

If you are a professional, an executive or manager, a mother or father with too much to do on your plate, plagued with worries, work and obligations, these tools will help you find balance in your personal and professional life, and guide you to stiller waters.

If you are a health-care practitioner, a medical professional, a pastor, therapist, probation officer or in a service industry helping people, you will find powerful tools to assist your clients, administer healing in your practice, and perspective to offset any of your own feelings of being overwhelmed.

If you are facing a significant health challenge such as cancer, if you are going through a divorce seeking to put the past behind you, or if you have recently lost a loved one, you will find concrete tools to ease you through your grief and bring solace to your heart. You will find healing and hope, lightness and renewal that will allow you to move forward with more joy and connectedness.

If you are an artist, wordsmith, an educator, student, social activist, peacemaker or creator who is experiencing uncertainty, these tools will free you from the ebb and lead you to the flow. They will awaken your vision and voice, opening up new pathways for your creative endeavors, inspiring you to move into a fuller and richer life.

Journaling, meditation and relaxation, are only ideas and intellectual concepts until you experience them for yourself. *When you experience them, you embody them.* Then your personal experience resonates and sounds a chord to your friends and family in an expanding circle around you. Don't be surprised if they, too, then want to explore these life-affirming practices. The practices, stories, meditations and quotes in this book are designed to support you in living a life of creativity, peace and joy.

A Word About Journaling

What journaling does for you

Journaling de-clutters your life

In a non-invasive way journaling assists you in excavating the stuff that has kept you stuck, *(but only if there is stuck stuff.)*

I've often said, the empty page is like God. It can hear anything, it can take anything, and it can handle anything. *(There are no mean judgmental Gods or Goddesses in my world.)* The blank page is a safe place to dump the trash so you don't carry it around in your head, heart, body, mind or soul. It's also where you can begin to hear all the compassionate voices that want to assist you and long to be set free.

Journaling allows you to dream on paper

In journaling, you dream stories that want to be heard or birthed into existence, the deep desires that are of the heart.

Some philosophies say not to have desires. I say have them. They can be your paths to creativity. For some, they are paths to God. Journaling is like dreaming on paper and it can show you *Your Way*.

Journaling clears paths to your own true voice

Through journaling you meet inborn strengths that can help guide you in your next adventure or in times of need. You bear witness to your own wisdom and to the gems that uplift your life. Through journaling you can learn to hear your own voice clearly. And it is your voice that can shine a light of transformation for you, that can be a message of transcendence to you, for others or the world.

Journaling lets you play with language and paint with words

In journaling you improvise, experiment, and play with your ideas and dreams on paper. *(Yes, play is worthy and majorly important in any creative venture. I know majorly is not a word, but I like it. It's one of my words.)*

Not the kind of writing you did in school, the tedious kind with someone breathing down your neck about correct grammar, paragraphing or syntax, but creative writing and journaling, the fun kind. For writing or journaling can take a variety of forms: letters, lists, scribbling words in little bubbles circles, made-up words, in symbols, pictures, color, paint, free-associative writing and dream-writing. Even defining words in any way you want to create new languages.

As I've told several adults, and one young child who was worried about keeping the words between the lines, "You can write on the walls if you want." Might not have pleased his mother, but you get the gist.

Journaling unveils the goodies that lay inside you

You find hidden reservoirs of creativity, designs and projects waiting in the wings of your life. You discover the stories that enrich your life. Secret dreams and ideas that want activation are set free. (Excavate, then activate!) You are now in touch with original inspiration, energy and excitement. You know the steps to take to continue to expand and unfold your creative genius … that are and were the keys for beginning any creative endeavor.

Journaling

Journaling heals loss

Journaling invites joy

Journaling reduces stress

Journaling speeds healing

Journaling creates clarity

Journaling promotes focus

Journaling enhances creativity

Journaling encourages innovation

Journaling brings ideas

Journaling assists organization

Journaling develops intuition

Journaling deepens peace

Journaling increases compassion for your Self

Your compassion for yourself supports Universal Peace

Journaling shared doubles the joy

What's Meditation?

Meditation is an ever-deepening investigation into silence
The Great Silence where peace reigns supreme

Meditation is a thoroughly integrated art and science, long in history, with valuable implications for our world. The following conversation between a businessman and myself scratches the surface, and is enclosed at the beginning of this book to give the reader only a brief understanding. A relaxation or contemplative practice like meditation will support your journaling, your creativity, and peace. Meditation is a lifelong practice and study. I encourage you to give it a try and explore it for yourself.

TK: My world is science, and ten years ago I would have told you that things like meditation and relaxation are bunk. But through my investigation with technology and tools like biofeedback, I started to have different experiences and wanted to know more. So talk to me about meditation.

EW: We are not our thoughts. We are not our feelings. We are not our perceptions. We are not our bodies. We are not our work, circumstances or finances. All of these conditions constantly change. So if we are not all these, who are we? What's the foundation of our life?

What are we? Where are we going? What is our purpose? Meditation is an exploration into what is behind all this that constantly changes. Is there a peace that passes all understanding? Does unconditional love exist? Where does creativity come from? Meditation is an ongoing investigation into the silence.

TK: Well, how does one do that?

EW: There are a zillion ways into the silence. Through observing the breath, with sound, words, mantra, prayer, contemplating a flower, staring at the stars, walking the beach, singing or studying a Zen koan, guided imagery, and mindfulness practices, these are all tools. There are as many ways as there are individuals or groups or organizations that want to learn. Meditation is not based in religion or on any religious practice although it can serve a religious practice. Whether you believe in Jesus, the Buddha or yourself, a mustard seed, your child, science or evolution, whether you're an atheist or fundamentalist, Democrat or Republican, if you believe in a God or not is irrelevant. Meditation is beyond all that.

TK: Sometimes I have all this data running through my mind and I seek to coalesce it.

EW: Yes, meditation provides the space to do that. There is a quote from a Scottish physicist that says their greatest discoveries occur in the three B's, the bed, the bath and the bus.* After hours and days of research, it is when the mind and thoughts are relaxed that the great discoveries are made. We are so accustomed to thinking with

---

After periods during which one has actively tried to solve a problem, but has not succeeded, the sudden right orientation of the situation, and with it the solution, tend to occur at moments of extreme mental passivity... A well-known physicist in Scotland once told me that this kind of thing is generally recognized by physicists in Britain. 'We often talk about the Three B's,' he said, 'the Bus, the Bath, and the Bed. That's where the great discoveries are made in our science.'
—Wolfgang Kohler

our linear minds that we get stuck in old grooves. Those grooves recycle old patterns of thought and rely on only half-information. When we are relaxed in bed at night, in the morning fresh from dreams, or just lying in the grass, that's when the information has time to rearrange in our brains. The result of this relaxation is the *Ah Ha* moment when creative genius strikes and you come up with a gem of inspiration, fresh ideas, and brilliant discoveries. It's because all of you – all your experiences, what society has framed as your "conscious thought", your unconscious, and super conscious – have the opportunity to get involved. Meditation provides that kind of focus where the big picture is seen.

TK: I call that the Eureka moment!

EW: Sleep and dreams give you opportunity to coalesce information in a way you didn't see before. Sometimes all we need to do is decode the symbols. Imagination is key, which also gets rejuvenated by rest and activated by dreams. Your creativity expands. This also occurs with meditation. In fact deep meditation is equivalent to many hours of rest. There are hundreds if not thousands of studies out there about the wonders of meditation not only in terms of creativity, but also in terms of medical science and the immune system.

Solutions to problems, creativity, and healing all happen in the in-between, in the space between what was and what will be. The possibility for something new to be born lies in the unknown because there is a relaxation from the holding patterns of what we thought and the holding patterns in our cells. When this holding, tension or pressure, contraction and constraint are finally released it is as if a wave of energy swells and returns. Expansion occurs and new insights are seen. There is more breath, more aliveness, and more vitality, which allows the body to marshal its forces in a different way than before. Balance returns. This is the *Grace of the Unknown*. I would wager to say this that exists, in what I refer to as spaciousness, is wholly and holy alive. It lives in us and through us. It is with us at all times. It is both ancient and familiar, but simply forgotten. Meditation aligns us to this, to this space, to this unknown, to this grace, to this silence and peace and love.

So, you see there are many benefits to meditation. It also sharpens the focus but in a way that is open, or in an open system not closed. Our senses even work with the spaciousness. They open and close accordingly. When it's dark outside and our visibility is less, our hearing becomes more acute. Everybody hears sounds in the night. And the drip of water that you didn't hear during the day drives you nuts when you shut your eyes to go to sleep.

TK: Yes, I love the story about the man who lives by the train tracks. Every night the train comes and he sleeps soundly. One night the train doesn't go over the tracks and he startles awake and says, "What's that?"

EW: Yes, what is this Great Silence?

TK: How does this apply to organizations?

EW: Well imagine you get an organization or group of people actively meditating together. Now imagine that you introduce questions into this process that help them focus on their strengths as an organization, on what they'd love to create, on the bigger picture, on how they can reach or meet their goals. What happens is that what is considered a problem dissolves. It becomes a non-issue. You're so focused on what can be, on what you're creating, that what wasn't or what didn't happen disappears.

TK: I'd call that focusing on the opportunity present instead of the problem.

EW: Exactly. The other scenario is that the gift of the perceived problem comes into alignment with what you're moving towards and then serves the bigger picture. Your staff is happier and your clients are happier. Health increases in that kind of an environment. Absenteeism decreases and the group's enthusiasm is enhanced. Everyone gets more energy through the process and you get the best minds working towards the collective goal of the organization, while serving individual needs by relying on and bolstering their strengths.

TK: Well how do you do this?

EW: For example you ask them to describe a time when they felt relaxed and at peace, what were the conditions of their life at that time? How did their body feel? Then you ask them to describe a time when they felt totally heard and listened to and in the flow with their creativity at work.

TK: Yes, I think I'd phrase it like this, *"Describe a time in your life when you were so relaxed that your creativity flowed?"*

EW: Perfect. I'll use that.

TK: Write it down.

EW: Then you get them aligned around that with action and a plan they can focus on. I was speaking with a friend recently and we talked about where we are trained to focus. Often our focus is small, it's on the problems, and that causes us to dive. When you turn it around and pick your head up out of the sand, you see that your Knowing is much greater than where your focus has been.

We live in a culture where we have created a language of deficit: dysfunctional, problem-solution, debt-based society, attention deficit disorder, co-dependent, and on and on. And our language creates grooves in our brain.

TK: Yes our words create neural pathways.

EW: Glad you're in the sciences! So imagine if we introduced this kind of questioning and inquiry to an organization, with language that is uplifting and possibility-focused? Now imagine it is anchored and enhanced with meditation.

TK: Wow. And it's not just for the new age.

EW: Right. It's for the justice system, our CEO's and boardrooms, government organizations, the military, our hospitals, and health care workers. I've had this vision since the early nineties and now you see the seeds sprouting and breaking ground.

TK: There's a lot of possibility there.

EW: My point exactly! Lots of room for exciting growth – just imagine.

Your Sankalpa

Sankalpa is a Sanskrit word that means resolve. It is akin to an intention, which I like to think of as being *in tending* to, as in nourishing. A Sankalpa can be a positive thought or even a prayer that can be created for a specific situation or outcome, or for your life as a whole.

It is not necessarily an affirmation though it can be one. It is not something like, I am now quitting smoking, or I am becoming a better person. Because your Sankalpa is not a statement of personal will. Rather the Sankalpa comes from your Spirit and your greater humanity.

Here are examples:

My Sankalpa is

» To allow play to be the center of my life
» To allow my creative voice to be divinely inspired
» To walk in faith with courage
» To be enlightened
» To be a bearer of peace
» To be of good cheer
» To provide a beautiful life for my family

» To alleviate world hunger
» To alleviate poverty and sorrow
» To be kind
» To remain open-hearted and go with the flow of life

Even the Serenity Prayer can be a Sankalpa –

> *Grant me the serenity to accept the things I cannot change, courage*
> *to change the things I can, and wisdom to know the difference.*

As you begin using this book, write down a Sankalpa for yourself. You can write your Sankalpa for a specific body of work you are creating, a short-term endeavor or trip you are taking, or you can create a Sankalpa for the duration of your life, a life Sankalpa. Your Sankalpa may immediately occur to you or it may develop over time.

One way to develop a Sankalpa is by remembering a time or place when you felt peaceful, when everything felt right in your world through every fiber, pore and cell of your being. You can invoke this sense of peace right now through your breath by relaxing into your body, or reading through and using the sensory meditation on page 35.

If there are strong, uncomfortable emotional components in your life at this time, like a fear or sorrow, anger or negativity, ask yourself what is the opposite of that and bring that to bear on your Sankalpa.

When you have a sense of peace, ask yourself what other experience is there? Is there a feeling of comfort, contentment, kindness or joy? Where in your body do you feel it? Then whisper, what is my Sankalpa? And wait.

Notice, without interpretation, any images or words or feelings that come up. If nothing appears then just keep listening to your body. If words or images are bubbling forth directing you to your Sankalpa, then ask a few more questions.

Is my body comfortable with this Sankalpa? Does my body say, *Yes*? Is there a sigh or a sense of relief in my belly and heart? Is this Sankalpa resonant with my values, my beliefs, and my dreams?

Then ask yourself, when this Sankalpa is fully alive in me, how will it affect my life? What would I know about myself that I didn't know before? What would I gain that I didn't have before? How would I feel? How would I think? How would I act? What kind of freedom would I experience? How would I move in my life differently?

Then take your pen and paper and bring forth the images, feelings, words and sounds, into simple, present tense language. For example,

> *My Sankalpa is to be playful in my work.*
>
> *My Sankalpa is to feel grateful for all that I have, all I am blessed with, and all that I am.*
>
> *My Sankalpa is to know where I am going in a secure, centered way.*
>
> *My Sankalpa is to be relaxed with a peaceful easy feeling, happy in my world.*

If no words come, then record the image.

> *Light and a pool of water before me that is warm and inviting*
>
> *A butterfly landing on a rock in a desert storm.*

Ascribing words to what you know in your heart is not necessarily what is important. Images are just as powerful. More than image or word, it is the *feel of your Spirit's Knowing* that is paramount. Recognizing the feeling will deepen any creative endeavor. Images and words are the tools used to convey this feeling to yourself or another. They are touchstones that anchor your recollection of what it is that you choose to feel or what it is that you are in attendance to.

You are also not married to what you choose for your Sankalpa. You can change it tomorrow. If nothing comes to you, it's okay not to have a Sankalpa. If you want one, simply create the intention to have one. Wait for the time to ripen and one will show itself.

If you wish to create a longer Sankalpa in any form, poetry, song, collage or prayer, feel free. The following example is a longer poetic Sankalpa that expresses one monk's resolve to love, to serve, to live, to give.

The Sankalpa of Paramahamsa Satyananda Saraswati

I am an invisible child of a thousand faces of love,
That floats over the swirling sea of life,
Surrounded by the meadows of the winged shepherds,
Where divine love and beauty,
The stillness of midnight summer's warmth pervades.

Life often cuts at my body and mind
And though blood may be seen passing,
And a cry might be heard,
Do not be deceived that sorrow
could dwell within my being
Or suffering within my soul.
There will never be a storm
That can wash the path from my feet,
The direction from my heart,
The light from my eyes,
Or the purpose from this life.

I know that I am untouchable to the forces
As long as I have a direction, an aim, a goal:
To serve, to love, and to give.
Strength lies in the magnification
of the secret qualities
Of my own personality, my own character
And though I am only a messenger,
I am me.

Let me decorate many hearts
And paint a thousand faces with
colours of inspiration
And soft, silent sounds of value.
Let me be like a child,
Run barefoot through the forest
Of laughing and crying people,
Giving flowers of imagination and wonder,
That God gives free.
Shall I fall on bended knees,
And wait for someone to bless me
With happiness and a life of golden dreams?

No, I shall run into the desert of life with my arms open,
Sometimes falling, sometimes stumbling,
But always picking myself up,
A thousand times if necessary,
Sometimes happy.
Often life will burn me,
Often life will caress me tenderly
And many of my days will be haunted
With complications and obstacles,
And there will be moments so beautiful
That my soul will weep in ecstasy.

I shall be a witness,
But never shall I run
Or turn from life, from me.

Never shall I forsake myself
Or the timeless lessons I have taught myself,
Nor shall I let the value
Of divine inspiration and being be lost.
My rainbow-covered bubble will carry me
Further than beyond the horizon's settings,
Forever to serve, to love, and to live
As a sannyasin.

The Sankalpa is yours. There is nothing you have to do with it. It will show up in the quiet moments of your life and seep down into the spirit of your bones. It will act as a guiding force. As a subtle suggestion and request from yourself to yourself, that will help you gently lean into your vision for what you would love to create in your life to lift you up and up and up.*

---

* Further information on Sankalpa and the work of Swami Saraswati can be found at www.saraswatiyoga.com/Sankalpa.html

Journaling Through Grief

Your powerful story-words hold seeds of brilliance to what ails you. Your visionary qualities and the best of your stories, even sorrowful ones, contain access points for healing and creativity.

Keeping a journal is cathartic. It unburdens you from your woes, lifts you in times of grief, and helps release what no longer belongs in your life.

Not all people come to journaling through pain, but many do. There are several studies that report the healing benefits of keeping a journal. When people write about their stress, crisis, illness and dis-ease, recovery time is reduced and healing is speeded. Even if writing feels uncomfortable at first, after an initial period of writing, suffering and grief subside.

William Shakespeare said it best when he wrote:

> *Give sorrow words. The grief that does not speak whispers the o'er fraught heart and bids it break.*

A long time ago an actress friend of mine said, "Pain is pain, whether it is a pinprick you suffer or a broken leg. At the end of the day, it's still pain." She didn't differentiate between the degrees that people suffer. Her heart was compassionately open to all levels of anguish people endure. And so, too, grief is grief, and loss is loss, whether you have lost a beloved, whether you are in-transition between jobs, moving from one home to another, whether you have lost your health, your sense of purpose, or are grieving the devastation of war. I tell the people in my classes to write. I cannot explain the phenomena except to say it works. I tell them the empty blank page is like God, able to hear your every word and thought, feeling and prayer. Capable of turning tears into strength, sadness into laughter, sorrows to joy.

Grief is an emotion that needs a witness in order to heal. What that means is that you need to find someone or something that hears you or that you feel hears you deeply. That accepts and sees you in your grief, with love. Having a witness provides you with an avenue and means for releasing the sorrow, the grief, the anger, the burden, the worry and fear, the loss and the tears. Holding it inside so very close to one's heart without a witness keeps you locked in loneliness and "whispers the o'er fraught heart and bids it break." Having a witness helps you to see your way out of the darkness.

Grief is an emotion that needs some form of expression. The form of expression and even the witness can be words on a page, a story, a poem or song, paint on a canvas, singing to a tree, carving a stone or talking to God. I know two women whose husbands were tragically killed in separate motorcycle accidents. One opened a store after her husband died. The other woman launched a non-profit. After my father passed from cancer, my brother became interested in learning about alternative cancer treatments. During the next ten years he researched and then launched www.latestagecancer.com serving to disseminate information for those diagnosed with late stage cancer, offering alternatives and hope.

You can pen a book, shoot a film, or build an empire and create something, anything, to serve others in their time of need and to remind yourself that in your grief you are not alone. In journaling you do not die with your feelings of loss, but slowly they are transformed so something beautiful may grow from your pain.

> *That's the way writing often starts, a disaster or a catastrophe of some sort, as happened to me... And I think that's the basis for my continued interest in writing, because by writing I rescue myself under all sorts of conditions, whatever it may be that has upset me, then I can write and it relieves the feeling of distress.*
>
> —William Carlos Williams

A Cathartic Writing Example

I'm angry. It's like my bones are on fire, which causes me alarm. Will it bring harm? Or by writing will it release the far cooling winds to restore my peace because that is ultimately who I am, who we are, who you are.

I feel burdened down by the weight of wood and coal and no oxygen to breathe and I have to be fire chief with hose. But even writing that, that I have to be fire chief with hose, brings relief. I know this because I sigh. I have hated something these last four months. Not someone but a situation. Hated. It isn't a word that I fear. I understand hate and the fantasy to hurt and harm. I do, and maybe my repugnance at violence is that it still lives in me. My abhorrence: the desire to see peace rise instead and to deliver a deathly blow to the ugly and impure.

People think I am peaceful and I am by nature
a peaceful person, but this does not mean I
don't travel to the dark side not usually by
will but circumstance that makes me feel
like a fiery wiry crazy out of control bitch.

The thing is, peace draws me back to her side
again and again, like the pen. Like the pen, like
water that I must drink and excrete, and swim
about in, I am drawn willingly with no control
and this is wisdom that pours from my soul,
savior queen, Goddess, Universal Divine.

It is quite something to be known by this Universal Divine and to be part and parcel of Her Design
in an intricate web and for a great service and
cause. It is quite something that brings release
and relief. It is the only thing I can hold onto, this
knowingness that I am a part that is known by
Her or Him. That I rest in God's Design unconditionally accepted and loved. Rage, grief and
violence is not condemned or judged but seen
and heard without the discontent or malice that I
would personally spill upon it thereby mounting
the inferno. In this unknown Grace, in this seeing
acceptance I rest and am freed. No worries, nothing to do, no debt, no responsibilities, no ugly
harshness, no guilt, no burden or shame, no holding of past or even anticipated future pain. No
nothing, peace. Just peace and relief, a return of
the Beloved to my heart, to my body, here and now.

The fan of the flames then dies, my bones
cool. There is stillness in the air. I breathe
peace. I breathe peace. I breathe. Peace.

I include the above cathartic writing as an example to say take heart. Be not afraid if you do feel, write, and pour the fallout of explosive emotions on the page. It is safe. When I wrote the above piece, in the very second of writing, I knew there were harsh sounding sentences that were simply not true. But the dramatist (and maybe the melo-dramatic dramatist) checked in at that time and lightly took hold of the pen. I could have gone back and adjusted the sentences as soon as I finished those very sentences. But what was written did not scare me. *In that past moment there was an emotional truth and energy of agitation that was finding its way to freedom through the act of writing.* This I accepted. It is this acceptance that makes such writing safe and cathartic. This acceptance is what brings release and relief.

If strong feelings and thoughts seem to ravage you without control, and you express them through personal cathartic writing, with total compassion, it gives way to peace. The temporary insanity or what we would personally condemn in ourselves or another finds its way into a larger container. In the spaciousness of that large container, there is room for the feelings to morph and change, breathe and rearrange. Thoughts and feelings are sorted out and restructured, the body is reassembled, and we effectively put ourselves back together in a new way.

However personal cathartic writing is exactly that: personal. I do not take it as permission to send raging maniacal letters to people I feel may have hurt me, or whom I harbor anger towards. I sort through my stuff first. If there is a need to express discontent, I try to find words that specifically convey what I'm searching to express without blame. Because in my world we first and foremost live in a circle of peace, and peace is what I am ultimately after.

Call it a world of peace, an ocean of peace, a womb or a cave. It is a peace that is always present, ever in and around us. It is ultimately where we come from, who we are and where we're going. When we feel lost in a rush of anxiety, fear, worry, sorrow, grief, anger or rage, we know we are still safe because there is this ocean, circle and world we live inside and that lives inside us that we can anchor to at anytime. We reach out and up or in and down, or simply sit still and touch peace, our eternal ultimate essence.

This knowing allows me to pour troubles or distress onto the page, and it helps lead me home restored and renewed to my Self. Like a shaman who retrieves missing parts, writing does the same thing. It re-stories your cells and yourself. You are able to feel the warm fires that nourish and light your way. You are able to remember your own peace, and refill yourself with that peace, with silence, wonder and glory. This knowing is a gift. Journaling is safe. It is the dock for when you feel adrift at sea. It is the star in the sky that can lead you to shore.

The practices on the following pages are basic for any journaling aficionado because they are simply writing. Do not feel you have to write cathartically as in the example. To "give sorrow words" is an option if you are feeling deluged by upsets, overwhelmed by work and stress or grief, challenged by relationships, or overcome by the evening news. Cathartic writing can be healing and it is one aspect of writing available to you, but not a requirement of the journal process. Neither should you feel that you have to drudge up a sorrowful past in your writing unless it serves you in some way. Difficult experiences may influence your life, they may even, in part, give shape to your life, but by no means do they define your life. For there are also infinite rooms of creativity, expansion and peace, waiting for you to enter into through the journal and your written words on the page.

Journaling Basics

Practice I: Getting started

The Basic Journaling Practice is easy. Simply write about anything at all, past, present or future. It does not have to be cathartic or it can be.

Natalie Goldberg, author of *Writing Down the Bones*, suggests setting a timer for ten minutes and writing non-stop. No crossing out, no editing, no correcting grammar, no stopping.

Julia Cameron, author of *The Artist's Way*, calls it *The Morning Pages*. She suggests that you write three pages every morning. Like brushing your teeth, it clears the palette and you are free to move into your day with a greater sense of lightness and freedom.

My suggestion is for you to write, be it ten minutes or three pages, morning, afternoon, night or whenever you can carve out uninterrupted time for yourself.

Get a pad of paper, sit down and write. This is journaling practice. If you get stuck, then keep going by writing the last word you wrote again and again. Or write the entire last sentence again and again or doodle.

Years ago when I worked a temporary boring desk job, I took a piece of paper and simply wrote the words, *Lead me to the Source, lead me to the Source, lead me to the Source.* I wrote that line over and over and over again. The next thing I knew the pen took off, *Lead me to the Source of all magical wonder, beyond the fighting, beyond the thunder.* A children's story emerged. I shared it with a mentor and she asked, "Can you write another?" I answered without hesitation, "I don't see why not." I have no idea what gave me that kind of bravado, but I went home and wrote another story that night. Over the course of the next few months several more stories poured out. That is when I purchased my first computer and began to organize and sculpt the words. Such is the power of sticking with a single sentence or word.

If you think there is nothing left to say and your pen suddenly wants to stop, then bring yourself into the immediate present moment by noticing your breath. Then, write down your observations of where you are sitting: the surface you are writing on, the grain in the wood of the table where you sit, a reflection in the glass of what you see, the humming sound of the refrigerator you hear, the temperature in your feet, how your hand feels gliding across the page. Simply describe and describe simply the present moment.

> *Describe something just as it is.*
> *Do not worry if it is angular and clumsy or how it comes out.*
> *Just look at something and put down what you see.*
> *Remember William Blake, who said:*
> *"Improvement makes straight, straight roads,*
> *but the crooked roads without improvement*
> *are roads of genius."*
>
> —Brenda Ueland

It's that simple.

Practice II: Word prompts

Writing engages body, mind and heart. It takes you into uncharted territory of your imagination. More importantly, it is fun. When I teach journaling to enhance creativity, reduce stress and deepen peace, I have a magic word-box. People choose random words and then they create sentences from them. The sentences don't have to make sense. In fact, sometimes the fun of it is that the sentences make no sense at all. Instead they create pictures in your head or ideas for stories, poetry, movies, books, song and art.

Sentences like, "The ranting banana climbed the hill skiing after the tired old monkey."

"Music is the key to my salvation even underwater where the apricots grow."

One day in class, as I opened the word box, a young woman asked, "What does this do?"

"Nothing," I chuckled, "except to invite a sense of play using random words without thinking about grammar, syntax, and getting it right." As someone with rules and constriction in her life, she understood and immediately joined in. Journaling is not about 'getting it right' and neither is creativity. Knowing this actually frees you.

Finding word prompts

Write down five of your favorite words.

» Meander
» Water
» Smooth
» Creative
» Children

Write down five words that sound sensuous, weird or interesting to you.

» Luscious
» Slush
» Yummy
» Oxymoronic
» Supercalifragilisticexpialidocious

Write down five disturbing words.

» Violence
» Killer
» Destroy
» Bombs
» Wrenching

Write down five places.

» Seascape, landscapes, moonscapes
» Mother-in-law's rose garden
» Sunrise on the beach in Cypress
» Drinking coffee at 7:00 AM at Fifth Avenue and 34th Street
» Bach piano concerto at Carnegie Hall on Christmas Eve

Write down five qualities.

» Cantankerous
» Peaceful
» Blunt
» Sharp
» Inspirational

Write down any five words that come to mind. They do not have
to be related.

- » He-She
- » Pillow
- » Frozen
- » Dread
- » Pink

Look around the room you are in and write down five objects you see.

- » African statue of boy holding baby
- » Ceramic bowls
- » Winter coat
- » Green limes
- » Chess pieces

Write down five more words, any words.

- » Music
- » Death
- » Beauty
- » Paint
- » Geraniums

And five more.

- » Cold
- » Laughter
- » Sheep
- » Crystal
- » Canvas

Take one of your word lists that you've just composed and begin writing, using some or all of the words. Or mix it up by choosing one word from each of your lists. Create your own lists: Baby's first words. Favorite foods. Luxury vacation wishes. Favorite names. Hidden places. Funny moments. Other worlds.

In addition to a magic word box, I have a box with phrases and fill-in-the-blank sentences for workshop participants to play with. One woman picked at random the word *Invitation*. The sentence that she happened to pick from the box, also at random, was: *Invite your muse in to stay in your home, your heart.* She explored what the word and sentence meant to her in the following piece.

> **When you issue an invitation, you make a choice. You are in control. You can open the door and let the muse in – or not. It is not an obligation. My, it's noisy in here. What is making that noise? That cell phone sounds like a cow mooing. It's very distracting. Ah it stopped. The Gods are good.**

> **Or not. Why would you choose not? What are you afraid of? Your muse is not a taskmaster. It is a playmate. Playmates are fun! They add to your life. Invite your muse in to play with you.**

> **That's it. Pick a comfortable spot. Sit down and play with your muse. Sit down to play, not work! Resolved: I will play everyday with my muse, my playmate. I need a name for my muse, my playmate. What name? Think about a name...**

Kathleen, the woman who penned the piece, was at first taken aback. She thought her words were a little too "all over the place." That is sometimes the nature of journaling. She started on a track, which changed when a cell phone rang, which changed again. She discovered that her muse wanted her to play with words – not work with words. The nature of play is a little all over the place. But within the seeming chaos, there is an order. Within the randomness of events or words or design there is sequence and a logic that may not, at first, be understood. The creator is the one who sees the connections, the logic, sequence, and order that others do not see. In this kind of play and vision we discover new realms of possibility. This vulnerability and willingness to play exercises our adaptability and adaptability is our sustainability. It is through being able to adapt that we live, grow and find new life. As a result of this exploration, Kathleen was able to approach her writing differently, penning stories that had been waiting for her to play with and pay attention to in this lighter way.

Word prompts and phrases are one way to play with words. There, if you choose to use them, but not a requirement. In fact the beauty of journaling is that there are no rules or requirements except the ones you make up for yourself in the moment.

Practice III: Writing the present moment

Write down what you observe around you.

>> What do you see? What do you hear?
>> What do you taste on your tongue?
>> What do you feel against your skin?
>> What do you feel in your bones?
>> What is the temperature in your home?
>> What is the weather outside?
>> How is your body sitting? What are you sitting on?
>> What is the texture and surface that you are writing on?
>> How does breath feel moving into your body?
>> How does your left big toe feel?
>> How is your right knee positioned?
>> What are the thoughts running through your head?
>> What are you feeling in your gut? In your heart?

When you feel like writing but don't know where to begin, start exactly and precisely right where you are now. Writing the present moment sharpens your awareness. You notice more. It relaxes you by bringing you into the present. It increases your sensitivity to environments in a healthy and detached way. This is because you get to observe and witness your environment, what you see, hear, touch, feel, taste, and observe without adding interpretation, meaning, reflection, and analysis. It's a great exercise, and both a healing and creative practice.

Writers across the board describe what they observe. *Cobbled streets filled with vendors selling bright red cherries. Overripe apples splayed on tables next to freshly-killed meat.*

It's a simple description. You can see red cherries, and everyone knows what overripe apples taste like, and maybe you can smell the freshly-killed meat or even feel disgust that overripe apples are displayed next to the meat.

In the book, *Women Celebrate: The Gift in Every Moment*, there is a story by a woman named Myrtle Archer called *"The Solace of the Wee of Life."* In it she describes how she dealt with her grief and anguish resulting from the murder-suicide of her in-laws. After doing all the chores, washing all the windows, any and every activity one can do to assuage grief, she started focusing her vision and gaze smaller and smaller to what she described as *"the Wee of Life,"* the ant crawling across a blade of grass, *"The symmetry of one cloverleaf entranced me as did a grain of salt in purest white on the yolk of my breakfast egg."* She wrote, *"The more painful the heartache, the smaller I, for a time, focus my gaze."*

The pure act of observation was what she could handle and was what slowly helped her heal. Such is the power of this great tool, the moment, the exact present now moment and the peace of that.[*]

---

[*] *The Solace of the Wee Life*, by Myrtle Archer, can be found in the book, *Women Celebrate: The Gift in Every Moment*, compiled and edited by Elizabeth Welles, published by Peace Communications.

Writing from the present to the past to the present

Grace, a woman who came to one of my classes, wanted to continue with the spiritual journal she kept but she also wanted to explore unresolved issues that kept creeping up in her life, her "problems" and "patterns," she said. I asked her to begin writing from the present moment, right from where she was. Noting her internal environment including how she was feeling, her body and breath, and also noting her external environment: the sound of the fountain, the people walking by, the blue sky, the color of the mosaics on the round table from where she wrote.

"Let the sounds of your breath and the fountain or how you are feeling in this moment take you into the dance of what you wish to explore," I told her. "Then from the depth of what you are exploring, write and spiral back to the present moment and to your own Presence."

She wrote for ten minutes, put down her pen, then looked up, smiled, and proclaimed, "You know, that was good. My problems aren't as big as I thought they were."

Writing from the present moment into a story or issue and then writing yourself back to the present moment is another way to gain clarity and perspective simply because you are not stuck in the rut of what you perceive as your problems. Instead you write towards them and then away from them to discover this moment, not the past or the future, just the simple and yet powerful now. Albert Einstein said, "You cannot solve a problem from the same consciousness that created it. You must learn to see the world anew." Journaling helps you see the word anew.

Zoe Murdock, author of *Torn by God: A Family's Struggle with Polygamy*, reveals how she got her name, while also speaking to the rich results received when she started writing from the present moment.

"I started using the name *Zoe* some years ago when I was writing in a stream-of-consciousness style that I've come to think of as 'mind-mapping.' I would start from an impulse in the present moment (usually an emotional roadblock in my life), then I would track that feeling back through time, moving through present and past tense, from 'third-person objective' to 'second-person accusatory' to 'first-person acceptance.' I always seemed to arrive at a point in my childhood where I would discover the source of the feeling. It was an amazing journey, not only of self-discovery, but it also taught me a tremendous amount about writing, the effect point of view has on a story, the power of tense, how the rhythm of a story can carry the reader along. So what does this have to do with my name? While I was exploring these mind maps, I could feel I was changing. I was tracking what I thought of as the essence of my life. Zoe means 'life' in the Greek language, so I took that name."

Writing is like having two lives. You get to re-experience the subject you are writing from a new perspective. This is because when you write about the past, the future, a juicy romantic affair, a job gone awry, the feeling of loss or love or inexpressible beauty, you bring to what you write your Presence. You bring your wisdom, your appreciation, your gratitude, your anger or rage or whatever it is that has graced your life since. You bring memory, reflection and interpretation that now contribute to your deeper insight and understanding. Even if that means you find no meaning, which can, in itself, be a powerful note and conclusion. Most deliciously, you bring your imagination, where you can delve into play with the fictitious. Even if what you write about really happened, you get to bring your mischievous muse, irascible, gentle or wise, who, if you are open, may spin your story in unusual fashion, and towards a different direction that you would not have originally scoped out or planned.

The Guest House

This human being is a guest house
Every morning a new arrival.
A joy, a depression, a meanness,
some momentary awareness comes
as an unexpected visitor.
Welcome and entertain them all!
Even if they are a crowd of sorrows,
who violently sweep your house
empty of its furniture,
still treat each guest honorably.
He may be clearing you out for some new delight.
The dark thought, the shame, the malice,
meet them at the door laughing,
and invite them in.
Be grateful for whoever comes,
because each has been sent
as a guide from beyond.

—Rumi

A Sensory Meditation Relaxation

Begin by closing your eyes. Relax your shoulders, and take a deep, slow breath and then release that breath slowly.

Soften your eyes, your jaw, your mouth, your tongue, and even the teeth in your mouth. Relax your shoulders and let your whole body soften as you breathe in and out. Have a sense of softness around your throat and your heart. Feel your body's connection to what you're sitting or lying down on: the chair, a bed, the couch or floor. Feel the connection of your hips, your shoulders and back, and continue softening.

Inhale a long, slow, deep breath and then gently exhale. Continue to soften the face, relaxing your whole body.

Bring your attention to your hands and fingers. Feel into your fingertips and notice the texture and temperature of your hands. Do they feel soft or rough? Cool or warm? Just notice fingers and hands. Now bring your attention to your feet and notice where your feet are. Are they in shoes, on the floor? Are your legs crossed with one foot dangling in the air? Notice the connection of feet to the surface they are on. Keep breathing long, slow and deep. Bring your attention to your chest area, your heart and your lungs, breathing in and out. Soften the whole body. Melt the whole body and relax. Soften all thought into your heart. Breathe and relax. Simply be. Keep softening and rest for ten minutes.

When it is time for you to return to consciousness, again deepen your breath, your inhalation and exhalation. Become aware of your fingers and hands and feet. Become aware of your skin and the air on your skin, the temperature and feel of air. Feel your body and whatever you are sitting or lying on. Become aware of any sounds around you. Breathe in and out, nice slow breaths.

Let yourself continue to feel the softness. When you are ready, open your eye and return to full consciousness.

The Voice of Compassion

Accessing Wisdom

I mark the age of seven as when my writing began. It began with diaries. I couldn't keep words on the line because at seven one's coordination of hand and eye and pen were not stilled enough. I couldn't spell correctly because at seven you're still learning the basics of spelling, grammar and syntax. But thankfully no one cared. I also discovered *The Voice of Compassion* when I was quite young, though I didn't call it that then. I remember there were times when I'd be feeling some discomfort and I'd invite into my heart all the other people in the world who were feeling the same thing. Later I learned that Buddhists had a similar practice. All I knew was that it made me feel better. All the people with the same thoughts or feelings or problem were in my heart with me and I didn't feel so alone. I also had the ability to write easily, and what I wrote never scared me. There were times when I would blast the page and let the words rip. After a while of writing in that ferocious way, there'd be a switch. I'd suddenly feel what I could only describe as *the inexpressible*. It would float in a kind of prayer. It was as if I were hearing the whispers of an unseen Presence. This Presence always responded with a clarity, wisdom, and compassion I had not known before.

I often experienced writer's trance when immersed in writing. Entrenched in the movement of pen to paper, fingers tapping against keys, with an outpouring of life into little visible symbols on the page, there was even rhythm to the breath as time stood still and hours passed unnoticed. A deep calm and peace prevailed. For me, it was and is the private sanctuary of my being, the sacred haven and space that has existed since I was a little girl.

As a child, I wouldn't be able to sleep until I wrote, or I'd awaken in the night *just to* write, and for years I recorded my dreams. I never thought of myself as writer, I just wrote. In fact if anything, I thought I couldn't write. When an assignment was given in school for a term paper, I'd panic and begin the project right away. The insights were startling to my teachers, and thankfully I had teachers who treasured that more than the organization on the page. I took one poetry class in college, got an "A" then stopped writing because I had no impetus to want to organize my writing at that time. I wrote because I wanted to, because it brought communion with myself, it brought peace. I didn't want to dissect or edit my writing. To the contrary I wanted to explore the inner realms of my being and its relation to the world I lived in. I allowed myself years of exploration before organizing the words in any fashion. The willingness to just write because I wanted to write was a lifesaver.

> *This is my essential reason for writing, not for fame, not to be celebrated after death, but to heighten and create life all around me... I also write because when I am writing I reach the high moment of fusion sought by the mystics, the poets, the lovers, a sense of communion with the universe.*

> —Anais Nin, from her Diary, 1939 – 1944

It was only at my grandmother's funeral, when I was in my late twenties, that I began to have an appreciation for my word's effect on others. My father asked me to read aloud a letter I wrote to him about my grandmother. Family wanted copies of it and asked if I ever thought of publishing. I hadn't. Years later, a co-worker in a book publicity firm said to me, "I don't care what you call yourself. If you're up at three in the morning writing, then you're a writer!"

Later, I taught journaling at a resort and spa in California where people from all over the world came to vacation. One result of my long meanderings with words and language, raw, natural and unschooled, is that I teach from a place of exploration, not evaluation. One woman who came to a class said, "Gee I always evaluate in my writing." But when I listened to the words she wrote and the words she spoke, I said "That's not evaluative, there's no judgment there. It's insight, perception and observation." She understood the difference and nodded in agreement.

There is nothing inherently wrong with evaluation. In fact at some point feedback and a discerning eye are welcomed, but when introduced too early, it kills the creative voice. People come to classes with enough baggage without forcing their hand and eyes in a way that divides their life even more.

> *Works of art are of an infinite solitude and no means of approach is so useless as criticism. Only Love can touch and hold them and be fair to them. Always trust yourself and your own feeling as opposed to argumentations, discussions or introductions of that sort. If it turns out that you are wrong, then the natural growth of your inner life will eventually guide you to other insights.*
>
> —Rainer Maria Rilke

The original title of the class was *Writing: Dreaming on Paper* because writing is in some sense like dreaming on paper. Immediate impressions and free-associative observations, thoughts, feelings and ideas pour down onto the page. Writing is not just a mental or intellectual process as some imagine it to be. Quite the opposite, this art and craft of the written word can be a deeply kinesthetic, if not sensual, even raw experience that later can become sculpted into a design that others recognize.

I would place small bottles of scented oil on the table for the participants to smell when they wanted a surprising fresh scent to stimulate the reptilian part of their brain to spur them to write, dream, heal, and create. Some people came to the class thinking it was an exploration into dreams. It was. More specifically than an exploration into the dreams that are dreamed in the night, it was an exploration into the dreams of one's soul.

At night we recapitulate the day's activities, subconscious desires and hidden fears. We both integrate and travel during the dark hours, and by morning we bring back awareness, vision, even prophecy. Gems are revealed and the future can be foretold. Writing is like dreaming on paper where words spill out at lightning speed with visions, fantasies, nightmares, and goals. What's left are the longings from your Soul.

But since there was some confusion, I changed the title to *Journaling for Well-Being & Peace*. Journaling to speed healing, reduce stress, promote focus, enhance creativity, develop intuition, and increase compassion for one's self.

People often come to spas in transition, and in the 'in-between' spaces of life. As sojourners on Earth, we are really here as visitors and therefore always in-transit. It is just that some transitions feel more pronounced than others. Some people walked into the class grieving the loss of a beloved spouse, parent or sibling. Some came having just experienced the loss of a marriage or job. Some came feeling the loss of control they thought they had on their lives due to illness, disease, or depression. And some came simply ready for retirement or a change in perspective. Every person, without exception, had a deeper need to hear the voice within and their own Creative Voice, and to what I referred to as *The Voice of Compassion*.

Joan, a highly creative woman, had lost all impetus to create until her therapists encouraged her to get out and explore classes again. She kept a journal of the day's events, but told me she wanted more from her journal. She wanted to see some sort of a progression. I asked her how she wrote – from a place of just recording the day's events or from her deep impressions and feelings intertwined with the experiences of her life? "Both," she said, "but something's missing."

I asked Joan to write a letter to herself from *The Voice of Compassion*. "What's that?" She asked. Now I know she knew the word, but it had obviously been so long since she had been in touch with compassion that I gave her some examples.

"It is the voice of absolute love. It is the voice that says, 'When you are hurt, let me hold you my child.' When you can't get out of bed, it is the voice that says, 'You are whole just the way you are. I am here, put your hand upon your heart and know I am with you.' It is the voice that says, 'You are loved and ever-loving.'"

Joan began to write and by the end of the session she said, "I don't know if I'll continue this, but I think what has occurred in my writing is that I've allowed this voice in a little bit, and I think this has the capacity to change my life." I encouraged her to write and journal about her art work, how her painting and work with clay and quilts made her feel. Before she left, she said, "I want to write a book about the creative person I was, and how I became separated from that, and the journey back to health and wholeness. This idea of compassion," she continued, "I never thought of it." Joan wanted to love and be loved and to feel compassion in her life. I told her she is loved and does love and that compassion already exists in her life. I generally did not give assignments but I told her to take this word 'compassion' as her assignment and to investigate it in her life. Joan didn't know if this would continue after the session, but seeds were planted, and she did continue writing. We ended up working together in several more sessions, and the seeds did grow.

One example of *The Voice of Compassion* reads as follows.

Dear One,

Answers are quiet and subtle. They do not respond to loud knocking and so sometimes when you ask, you hear back the response, "Peace Be Still." Pressing for answers with so many questions closes the answers that are right before you. For the loudness of sound makes elusive the answers. Answers are never answers in themselves. Answers are but guides, doors opening to show you one way, and answers in themselves will bring more questions, for there is no definite or definitive way about the roads upward. Silence in the Great Silence produces power to act, to see, to do truly for Me, and that means truly for you. For within the real you the answer stems and always in silence does it stem from. One petal of your rose, one petal is Silence, precious unadulterated silence growing you at times like these, in deep meditation. And whenever you can be sole with Me or doing for Me alone and with single-minded focus and attention, be it a dance or a speech or when you teach, when done with Me, the Divine in mind, there you will find the precious silence. One petal of your rose and from which it grows is silence, and in that silence you'll find your rest. Change is slow, deep, penetrating, effective; such is our way together my blessed, blessed child. Rest now. I am always with you. I will come again through the pen.

Another short example:

> **Rest, rest and be still. We see that you feel wor-
> ried, anxious, frazzled and tired. Rest your
> hands on your heart and know I am with you,
> rest and be in peace. You are not alone.**

Greta, another woman during the same session, had a unique set of circumstances. She wrote down only the negative things in her life, thinking it would help her. She discovered it didn't. Now for many, writing is cathartic and healing. In fact, studies show how writing through crisis helps one to heal faster, but this wasn't Greta's experience. She was stuck in a rut. I asked her why she wrote at all. She said because she thought she should, because that's what books said to do. I told her there are no "shoulds." If she didn't enjoy writing then there was no need for her to write. But there was more. She told me she had everything she wanted materially: security, marriage, job, but she felt that "inner" something lacking.

When I spoke of compassion her eyes filled with tears. I asked her to write a list of what she'd love to create. She cried as she wrote, telling me that she wrote out each line beginning with the words, "I'd love to create." Because she was afraid that her own "yeah, but" and "not possible" might stand in her way.

Things she couldn't imagine before appeared on her list, and things she knew she'd love to create appeared in a variety of new ways. Since there were a few people at this session, I chose not to work with her on the "buts" and "not possible," for that would take a different kind of exploration. Instead I suggested that she choose something on her list and write about the feeling it would bring her, exploring the quality she imagined would come from having her hands in clay, from taking a yoga class every day. She also had a fear of not completing things because she got distracted easily and then came down heavy on herself. I suggested she find a yoga teacher with whom she could take a class with, who might allow her to do just the breathing in the class if that's all she was called to do. When I taught yoga I gave my students permission. That is one of the biggest things lacking in our lives. I gave them permission that if they were tired from having traveled or from having been up since 4:00 AM, or having just done too much, they could simply lie down, listen to the music, relax and breathe. For rest is a sacred act.

I suggested to Greta that she allow herself small amounts of time throughout the day to simply stop and do nothing, a few minutes here, five minutes there. I also suggested that she quite literally move her arms. Lifting them towards the sky she was to breathe in peace. Then letting her arms move towards the earth she was to press out what no longer belonged in her life.

Greta's face brightened. I told her not to ignore the voice that spoke to her in harsh tones. We don't want to shut it down in the closet. Rather we'd like it to become quieter, dissipating its strength in our lives. If she needed to give it voice then she was to allow it to speak, but only for a few minutes. She was to ask it, "Who are you? What do you want?" Maybe this voice would be of some service.

"What if it speaks in tones that aren't very nice like 'you're stupid, wrong, not good enough?'" she asked.

"Then dialogue with the voice on paper, and let Compassion speak on your behalf. As in, 'that's not acceptable, would you please speak from a higher perspective?' Do not let this harsh voice take you off track and speak to you in tones that are less than attractive. Then go back to what you are creating in your life, to what gives you energy, to what starts your engines at midnight and keeps you up till dawn. Return to the Creative. And if that harsh voice needs a permanent place, then stick it in a novel, a monologue, a painting or poem – and keep it there!"

Another woman named Eileen stopped in on another day to write. At some point I asked what she did for a living. She worked in a sheriff's office handling and cataloguing evidence and weaponry that had been used to commit crimes. She was good at her work. She was appreciated in the office, but she wasn't happy. She wanted a change from the vibrations of negativity and darkness that these instruments of crime had stored. Except that she had not a clue as to what she wanted next. She had a normal childhood and loved to dance and sing and play, but with no more verve than anything else she liked. She was extraordinarily insightful, had a delightful sense of humor, and loved to be of service to people. She also wanted something different with her journal. I suggested that she make specific kinds of journal entries for a few days. "First day make an entry simply about the physical environment you'd love to work in. Another day make an entry about the emotional environment of your workspace, what kind of support you would receive and give. A third entry might tell you about the intellectual stimulation that would surround you."

She was on the verge of tears, half-apologizing that she didn't know why she was tearing up. It was normal I told her. "You are being heard and recognized for your awesome gifts."

She laughed and said, "You know I tried that gratitude journal they talk about but it didn't work for me, everyday it's the same five things I'm grateful for." Although Eileen couldn't get past the same five things she was grateful for and felt badly about that, she did speak about what she appreciated in others. So I told her to keep journal entries about what she appreciated in others. For the traits she appreciated in others were to be found in her own self as well. The beauty we recognize outside ourselves is often the beauty we don't see in ourselves.

Alice came to me for a private session, still grieving her father who had died years before. I had her write a letter to her father, and then I had her father answer her in a letter. How? You imagine your loved one sitting there beside you and speaking. You listen and write down their words. Writing letters to them and then hearing from them on special occasions or even over a period of time can bring comfort, love, insight, wisdom, and healing. This nurturing practice eased Alice through a period of delayed grief. Additionally, it helped heal the relationship to her father, even though he was no longer in the body. Finally, it freed Alice to move fluidly and joyfully in her present life.

Charlotte, another woman who stopped by to explore her life through journaling, was an extremely intelligent, highly verbal and organized woman who loved structure. Within a few years she would be facing retirement and she was also dealing with some health issues. She wanted an exit journal, a plan for how she would take everything she had gained at the spa to integrate it back into her life. We explored what she'd love to create in terms of health, healing massage, exercise and diet. I asked her to find qualities that embodied what she was creating, like *robust, alive, vital,* and *awake.* Since she wanted to focus on her body and become less of what she termed a "Type A" personality, I asked her to write *from her body.* It was a bit of a challenge because it was a new way of thinking for her, this thinking *through the body.*

Our short time together also included several suggestions for journaling regularly because she wanted to incorporate this into her life as well. So in addition to timed writing, setting a timer and writing for a predetermined amount of time, I suggested she write letters.

Letter writing is a powerful tool to articulate and express that which has never been expressed before. These are not letters to necessarily send, they are letters for the sheer sake of expression and for the revelation of the writer. It might be a letter of gratitude to a beloved grandparent who saw you with eyes of unconditional love, or a letter of love to your child. It might be a letter to a loved one who has died like Alice wrote, or a letter thanking your hands for the gift of playing the piano or holding a paintbrush. It might even be a letter to your own future self five years from now, or from your future self to whom you are today.

Finally, to give Charlotte a feeling of what it would be like to be a bit more integrated with her body, we called upon body-centered imagery. With it, she found a deep, restful peace. "This, the body, is where your guidance and answers will come from," I said.

Bounce

One young woman, age fifteen, stopped in to write. In her writing, she started with her future, skipped over to her brother, family, friends, college decisions, and school worries. She put down her pen, concerned that her writing was too bouncy.

"Bouncy," I repeated. I loved the word. "Stay bouncy, that's how it starts. So many people as they grow older hit the cement and smack, they thud and forget to bounce. We want buoyancy in our lives, perseverance without push, keep bouncing. How many people do you see who skip anymore?"

The other adult woman in class with two small children, smiled. She knew the difference between bounce and thuds. There are times in our work when it serves us to explore and bounce and meander and wander and find the joy of wonder without containing or hemming in the words. For many years I wrote with no direction for the words. I wrote because of love, because it was the time and place that I could describe my world and feel free. Freedom is when there is no ground under your feet. Freedom is when you soar and freedom is when you bounce.

If it is your path, there will come a time when at the urgings of your Soul, you will find shape for your work. The shape is the container, which allows you to find the fuller form for your creative self-expression. With your self-expression *formed*, your voice then finds its way into the world as a gift for a wider audience. Like rain pouring from the sky that finds the stream that runs to the river and gushes to the ocean to mix with the world.

Turning dross into gold

Jackie, another woman who stopped by to write, had so much disgust for her past that she hesitated to write down all the things she wanted to release for fear she wouldn't know how to return to some semblance of balance. Additionally she was afraid she wasn't at all creative. What occurred, instead, was a rapid spilling out onto the page that translated to truth, movement, clearing, and growth. She wrote about the disappointed relationships with men in her life, and then added a short poetic sentiment that metaphorically summed up her already poignant words. The poetry lifted her mundane experience into a form that allowed others to appreciate her experience. Moments before this woman was afraid she'd be left wallowing in self-disgust. But the very act of writing engaged her feeling body and she was able to move beyond the fear of wallowing that held her back. There was no analyzing or inspecting of what she wrote. There was no need. It was a simple release on the page, and creatively executed at that! After feeling the full force of what she wrote with both humor and tears, a veil was lifted and disgust was gone. Next she went on to write a most inspired list of what she'd love to create that astonished even her. It included painting, decorating her apartment with plants, different kinds of relationships, and working with children. Finally I suggested she write a love letter to herself. Turning dross into gold, she went for the gold. Balancing the dark with the light, her immediate transformation was an inspiration to all present.

Let the world be a mirror to you only in love

Often the people I worked with didn't have the support they needed, so I asked them to look for the *signs of support* that were there in other ways. Sometimes support seems to stand outside of yourself. Other times the supports seems to come from within. Whenever you receive support, wherever you receive support, allow it to become larger than the voice of negativity. You will discover affirmations in your life where you thought there were none. And always let the world be a mirror to you in love.

When a friend called, distraught, having just spent a $1000 on advertising for her business leaving only $20 in her pocket, she started saying how she had done so many things, knocked on so many doors. She couldn't understand why, in her eyes, her business and her life weren't working. Beneath her words lay self-flagellation. I stopped her cold. "Do not make yourself bad or put yourself down in any way because your business is not working and you are not making money. Do not think you did anything wrong. Do not let this world be a mirror to you except in love. Having a rough haul in your business, not enough money, and people not responding to your ads has no bearing on who you are, which is an enormously loving, vibrant soul, a steady rock to others in the storm. This world needs your Light. Go *deep inside* your heart and hear the wisdom there and know the love and joy and laughter that you are."

Invite creation and creativity in with its attendant compassion. Listen for the strong, clear, gentle and wise, still small voice within. It is always watching and witnessing, waiting for its turn to speak and be recognized. When the barriers to what it is you have craved for your entire life roll away, what supports you will become stronger than that which held you back, and there is a beautiful gift in the offing. A treasure that has always been with you and cannot ever leave you, it is the Gift of Self.

A preliminary optional practice:
Writing the distressed

Write down everything that's bothering you, any small annoyances that plague you or any large looming monsters in the dark: grief, sorrow, disgust, shame, anger, guilt, or remorse. *Write them down and get them out of your body and onto the page.* It may take any form. It may take the form of a letter – which you *do not send* if a situation, an environment, or another person or group of people are involved. Simply write and let the words rip into a letter or poem or journal note or list of whatever is robbing you of your peace. Write it out with feeling. Let your guts pour. You may even soak the page with tears. Then put the pen down and breathe deep breaths.

Intuitive wisdom practices:
The Voice of Compassion

Jot down a time or a list of occasions when you felt greatly received, unconditionally loved, or totally seen and accepted. It can be something very simple. Maybe you were being seen or heard by another person or maybe it was your dog that saw you, or a rock in nature, a Divine Presence or spiritual being. Write it down and recall the attendant feelings that accompanied this communion. Writing down memory of this kind primes the pump of feeling for this next part.

Now take your pen again and write "Dear (your name), then begin a letter to yourself from *The Voice of Compassion*. But here is the caveat – this voice *must* speak to you with unconditional love and kindness, very gently.

Let it tell you how loved you are. Let it share with you the love that lifts you above the problems that you perceive and face in your life at this time. Let it share with you the remembrance of your Soul and Spirit's dreams. Let it lift you up and reveal to you the greater perspective. Let it remind you of the larger playing field you live on. Let *The Voice of Compassion* tell you all you need to hear and know right now.

This voice will rescue you after you have had a challenging day. After you have done hard writing or written the things out that bother you, this kind voice will answer. And it is always there for you!!! This is an intuitive wisdom practice and this voice is one of your consultants. However it is not necessary to write down what plagues you first, because there may be nothing at all that burdens you. If not, write a letter to yourself anyway from *The Voice of Compassion*. It may share with you new insights or wisdoms long forgotten. It may share with you wonders from other parts of the planet or other worlds. Just listen to what it has to say and write, *to you.*

The Spirit of Peace

The Spirit of Peace or Lady Peace came one day to speak with one of my clients. The client wanted more peace. She told me she hired me because she sensed peace in and around me. I asked her to write herself a letter from her Spirit of Peace – and she did. *The Spirit of Peace* can be the same or different from *The Voice of Compassion*, a kind of cousin. You choose. And maybe they are the same and maybe they are different, at different times. In the world of journaling, you make the rules for yourself.

Name your voice

There are many voices rummaging around in our heads. There's the judge and the critic, the voice of that mean piano teacher you had in high school, there is the voice of your football coach, the voice of your mother or father or your spiritual advisor or priest.

But who was, and is now, the voice of total support, the voice of unimaginable love, inexpressible beauty, unsurpassable peace and unconditional kindness?

Create a list of names that you might consider calling your *Voice of Compassion*. You can name it whatever you want … *The Spirit of Peace* or your Rhythm of Truth or the Drum of Joy or your Cup of Peace or Joey or Pete or Jenn or Helen or Izzy or Crystal Lake or Emerald

Sky or Searing Blue Ocean. Or simply use *The Voice of Compassion*, or even the Ones with No Names. And then write a letter to yourself from that one, often!

Journaling with this voice provides you a way to directly reconnect to your soul, organize your thoughts, and regain balance. By writing to yourself from *The Voice of Compassion* and *The Spirit of Peace* you reweave peace from chaos, and discover *your voice* of authority. Not an authoritarian voice but the voice of *authorship*, you as author of your life, author of your ship, that you get to write and author and own.

Brenda Euland wrote, *"Think of yourself as an incandescent power, illumined, perhaps, and forever talked to by God and his messengers."*

The Voice of Compassion and *The Spirit of Peace* are God's messengers.

Meditation for Loving Kindness with The Voice of Compassion

Bring yourself to a beautiful space or a place of unspeakable beauty. It might be where you are right now, or it might be a place you have been before. It might be a scene that vividly unfolds before you in nature. In a palace of your design, in a rock garden or crystal cathedral, on this earth or in a world yet to be born. Go there and breathe.

In this place of beauty, soften your eyes and relax your shoulders. Feel your heart and solar plexus open to receive in the beauty that surrounds you, whether it is light and color, symphony and sound, or a feeling of harmony, peace and joy. Breathe the beauty through your pores as if your skin soaks and drinks, filling the cup of your heart with beauty and peace.

Let yourself feel surrounded by another presence or several other presences. Presence that is loving and warm and light. Maybe it's an angelic presence. Maybe actual people you know, maybe ancestors, people from your past or a great love from your future. Maybe otherworldly beings, earth Devas, the spirits of rocks and water and stones, or a Being like Buddha, Mother Mary or Christ.

The Presence or Presences you have invited give you plenty of space and are in a circle around you with unconditional support, unconditional compassion and love. The most profound and deepest acceptance you can conceive. And you are breathing this in.

As you breathe in, listen to their voices and hear what they sound like. Are their voices soft or loud? High pitched? Or do they speak in a low rumble? Maybe they sound smooth like chocolate, or perhaps their voice is not a voice but rather a light, color or texture that speaks to you.

Listen and hear what they are saying in whatever language they speak, and know that you understand. Among what they are saying, they are also speaking the words, "May you be peaceful, may you be happy, may you feel loved." Feel these words inside of you and then hear them inside of you as you say to yourself, "May I be peaceful, may I be happy, may I feel loved, may I be free." Breathe.

Look around and witness the unspeakable beauty. Look around at your friends. You see them and they see you. Feel into your heart and breathe in the pristine air you have created in this world. Then thank your friends for coming, and know they are always here for you whenever you need them.

As you breathe in, breathe this world into your cells. And as you breathe out, know this world and your friends are fully embodied in you, their love, their voices of compassion and peace, in this world of warmth and beauty.

Take a deep breath and feel yourself in your chair again. When you are ready slowly open your eyes.

And know this experience to be real.

Listening to the Wisdom Body

Listening is a simple and great forgotten art. It is a survival skill. You listen for when you are hungry and need to eat. You listen for when you are cold and put on a jacket. You listen for when to sleep, and when to be together with people or find time alone. You act on cues your body gives all the time for the basics: food, clothing, shelter, and relationships. All that need be done is that this wondrous listening, this kind listening, be generously extended out into all areas of your life. This listening is both ancient and familiar. It is a listening you have known all your life. It is a listening that sets you free.

This listening predominantly occurs through the wisdom of the body.

What is "body?" Body can be your body, your car's body, the earth's body, anybody and everybody, the feeling body, the physical body, the body of thoughts you have, your environment as body, and your home as body. The body as changing, unfolding, responsive and knowing is one partner in this journey of creativity.

If you stop and listen to the body, including your dreams and desires as body, it will tell you many things. It will especially make it easier for you to move in the direction of what gives you energy. For on this earth-journey, the body is home and hone. It is one of your directional signals telling you which way to turn and how to fly.

Know thyself

Deep listening is not rational to overly analytical figuring juxtapositions that confuse you by running rampantly through your thoughts night and day. Receptive listening is not entertained by the argumentative mind. Creators do not follow the template of what has come before. They listen and follow an *inner design* and they take actions based on this design. They practice the words, *Know Thy Self*. Creators are true to that Self, as best they can be, body, heart and soul. They know themselves and they know their world.

That is why Creators intentionally turn and tune their ears inward, away from the world. They initiate action based on inner knowing and intuition. What's so special about intuition? It helps you to make healthy choices for your life. It removes blocks, stagnation and obstacles naturally. It enhances your energy and guides you in creative directions that are aligned with your heart's desires and cherished values.

Inner knowing presents itself in a variety of ways, often speaking in whispers subtle as the wind. Knowing can come through the physical body and appear as the tightness of a clenched jaw, or in the hesitation or fluidity of your voice. It may appear as that gut feeling in the pit of your belly, or the melody your heart sings at the sound of a new idea.

Physical symptoms can be directional signals offering wise counsel if you listen. For intuition always comes with direction. However, there is a caveat. Listening and acting on your intuition does not necessarily mean that life will always go smoothly or that you will be without questions and enigma concerning your destiny.

David and Lisa

Sometimes we don't even know why we move in a particular direction. That is when trust or faith must be relied on and the words, *To Thy Own Self Be True*. It is as if a *Force* or *Energy* outside of our selves determines our behavior or even takes control of our physical bodies. Even though we ordinarily think we're in charge, making our choices and calling the shots, these are the moments that seem to stand outside of time when we must take heed to listen *even more closely* since there is no logical sense or precedence on which to rely. These are the times that are quite articulate and clear but remain a mystery because what is spoken is not spoken with words we initially understand. It is as if we must learn a new language, the language of the body in its broadest application.

David and Lisa paid a visit to a travel agent's office in India to design further plans for their trip abroad. During their meeting, David started to feel ill. By the time he and Lisa left the office, he was doubled over in pain on the busy Bangalore streets. Accustomed to observing and acting on the signs in their lives, he consulted with Lisa. Together they decided that maybe this trip wasn't right for them. They returned to the agent's office and apologetically cancelled the entire trip they had just mapped out. His mystery pain began to recede and he made a full recovery within twenty-four hours. David and Lisa did not know what the outcome of their decision to cancel their trip would be. They only knew how to act in the moment for that is all the direction they were given. It wasn't disheartening to them, but it certainly was quizzical. As it turned out, their vacation destination had been the region where the Tsunami hit in Southeast Asia. They did not consciously know this when they canceled their trip, but *Consciousness acting through David's body* did know this. He and Lisa simply chose to listen.

As it turned out they wouldn't have been traveling in the region at the exact time the Tsunami hit, but a few weeks prior. I believe time is skewed and changeable, a temporary illusion we use to organize our days. In light of time's fluidity, David's body was giving Lisa and himself plenty of breathing space for what would eventually occur during those few weeks. Sometimes you only need recognize that experiences that occur *in your life* or *to your life* may benevolently be *for your life*. Literally.

Intuitive knowing

Intuitive Knowing may come as a passing thought, in a vision or a dream, through a hunch, an instinct, or just plain common sense. Each person must learn how their own intuition speaks to them. It is a personal journey. A friend went to a tennis camp for a week, but when he arrived his racquets and sneakers didn't. They were lost in luggage hell somewhere between California and Arizona. Between calling the airlines, frantic and grumpy, he turned to me and said, "You know, last night I had this little passing thought, "Maybe I should wear my sneakers and put one racquet on the plane."

"That's intuition," I said.

"No," he said, "That's *not following* your intuition!"

It was such a quiet thought that he hadn't paid attention to it. Then, he went on to argue that if we don't follow every thought it doesn't necessarily mean the world will fall apart or something bad will happen. Well of course not, and that's why one must learn to distinguish when to heed the call and how your body speaks *to you, specifically.* Still I complimented him on having good intuition and then added, "All you need to do now is follow it." After hours of haggling on the phone, the bag arrived the next night, but not before he had to make several purchases that might have been avoided. Fortunately it wasn't a life and death matter like David and Lisa's situation could have been.

Events in the natural world

Sometimes this *knowing* can appear as a reflection outside of what we generally consider our own self or personal body. It can appear through the body of nature or through a communal body. Witnessing an event in the natural world, like a bird's flight, a deer's crossing, or the rain in a storm, can precipitate a sudden insight.

One morning I had a dream to visit a specific mountain in Colorado, and the dream said, "Come soon." I had never even heard of this mountain when I had the dream. I googled on the internet and found the existence of such a mountain in Colorado. Weeks later I was still thinking about it, turning the idea over in my head. It would take time away from the work I was engaged in, and it would cost money to go.

One afternoon I came home to find a small bird squawking just outside the gate to the entrance of my home. Every time I tried to get into the house, it screamed and jumped and tried to fly. I didn't know if its wing was broken, its foot hurt or if it had just gotten stuck, for it looked a little tangled in some vines. With all its struggling and squawking, I thought it might do itself more harm. I squatted to the ground and talked to it. "Look, I'm going to help you, but I have to get into the house. It's going to be okay. I'm not going to hurt you. I just have to move by you, okay?" Then I put my hand up and prayed out loud. The bird looked at me intently. As I walked by, its struggle quieted. Now, what was I to do? Call a raptor center – where? Call a vet? This wasn't something I wanted to deal with, but clearly there was no one else.

The bird brought back memories to all the birds my cats brought into the house, some of them still alive, when I was a little girl. There were cats in this neighborhood and I'd better get out there soon. I got a pair of rubber gloves, a small box in which to place the bird, and a scissor in case the little bird was indeed stuck on vines. As I opened the gate, the bird suddenly took off and flew up into the trees. I smiled at the creature, thinking, "You go girl!" I silently thanked God, and went back inside.

Later that afternoon I was sitting on my porch again musing about this dream to go to the mountain in Colorado when suddenly I thought of the bird. The direction was clear. The bird could fly. It just got its foot stuck – in front of my gate no less! It sounded like me, living in a small town year after year that I had gotten stuck in. I could leave and fly, too. I booked and took that trip to the mountains!

Knowing that comes to you through signs, through synchronicity, coincidence, through a sudden flash of intuition, or even dreams can look strange if you are used to acting on the premise that seeing is believing. But if you look at the body as a large container that holds your body *and* the body of life, then this kind of knowing becomes as natural to your world as the baby's breath. Like the sun's brilliant rays, intuitive knowing is clear, immediate and direct. It is available all the time, gracing every moment of life. It is only our awareness of it that is increased or decreased.

Listen to how your body speaks to you. Breathe deeply and feel a calm receptivity settle in your cells. Pay heed to whom and what enhances your energy, to what puts the sparkle of stardust in your eyes.

Then trust and take action based on that.

Writing from Your Wisdom Body

> *Listen to the past, future, and present right where you are.*
> *Listen with your whole body, not only with your ears, but*
> *with your hands, your face, and the back of your neck.*
>
> —Natalie Goldberg

By listening to the body and then journaling and writing *from the body* you can access intuition and tap into answers to questions that haunt you. Writing dialogue between two different body parts or between conflicting voices in your head can help you gain clarity and find direction in a playful easy way. I wrote the following piece when searching for answers on whether to return to school or not.

Why an MFA?

Great question. My heart and head battled it out.

For better or worse I'll call this first voice Heart.

> **Heart – Yeah, you've really missed intellectual stimulation these past many years. No wonder you want to go back to school.**
>
> **Head – Cool. Imagine what you could do with a Masters or Ph.D. in something, anything.**
>
> **Heart – Now don't get carried away, remember it's the intellectual stimulation and inspiration you want, mentorship and the opportunity to focus on a body of work and get started on a new one. There you go again with what it could get you. Remember the real inspiration for all this.**
>
> **Head – Yeah, but if you're going to do it, why not be smart and think ahead. You could teach, you could … well look at the prestige with those letters after your name. Finally you'll have the Masters or Ph.D. you said you'd never go back and get if you were out of college for three-plus years. So what if it has taken you thirty. Congratulations! Except that now your parents won't pay, but there's always financial aid.**
>
> **Heart – give me a break. Remember, you hate school. Love education, love learning, love knowledge, but hate school. And grades?**
>
> **Head – But you always got great grades!**
>
> **Heart – Yeah, remember you, the idealist? You hate grades. Good ones or not. That's**

one of the many reasons you didn't become
a formal teacher, you hate the system.

Head – Oh shut up Heart!

Heart – Don't be rude Head, you know I
know her better than you do on this one.

Okay, Okay, I shout, getting between the two of
them. So, are you telling me I should have done
this years ago? And who knows if I even want
to study writing. I like history (and have forgotten it all). I like biology and physics (and never
did study them), or maybe it should be something real useful for my life like rocket science.

Heart – And of course what if you just want
to take time off in the middle of it all, no time
off when you're in the middle of school. What
if you get a film or a show or a teaching gig?

Head – Yeah, no commitment.

Heart – And forget on-line study, you like live-
people – not computers! Just pursue your own
thing with that film director you've been working with and with your work as a monologist.
And then of course go back to teaching personal
journaling. You are the expert on that. Oy Gavult,
you've been doing it since you were seven!!!

Head gets kind of quiet.

I signed off:

Keeping the peace,
Eliz

It was a fun exercise that brought immediate clarity. I didn't go back to grad school and within a year I started to teach journaling to a much wider and larger audience.

Heart and foot

A client had surgery on her foot and was less than satisfied with the painful results. In fact she felt repugnant towards her foot. I asked her to pen a letter from her heart to her foot, a love letter. "A love letter?" she said. She wasn't sure she could do that and lightly resisted, but then dove in. The letter her heart wrote to her foot astounded not only her but her therapist as well. The insights her heart revealed cracked open a space where healing could shine. She ultimately found greater compassion for herself and her situation.

Heart and hands

Another client came to me with a habit of nervously rubbing her fingers together. She was embarrassed by her "obsessive compulsion," as she called it. But I said, "Let's look at it as your private ritual." I explained to her that the hands were an extension of her heart and that her heart wanted to express through her enormously creative hands much more than they had expressed up until that point. The hands are also a receiving point for our heart. They grip, they hold and they release like the heart that receives, carries and lets go. Together we did a sensory-visual meditation connecting her beautiful open heart to her creative extending hands. I didn't have her resist the motion of her fingers nervously rubbing together, but actually asked her to investigate what it felt like to rub them together, how the texture of her hands felt, the temperature in fingers touching, the line of energy that ran from heart to fingers to world. Within a few minutes, her hands simply relaxed, as did she.

Body dialogue

Choose two different parts of your body or even two different body symptoms.

Example

» Your heart and your hand
» Your heart and your head
» Your legs and your arms
» Your lungs and your knees
» Your gut, your heart, and your head
» Your liver and your intestines
» Your kidneys and your tongue
» Your hair and your nose
» A tickle in your throat and that scratch on your chin
» Your hiccups and your right big toe

Give them each a voice and record their conversation.

Luz, a student in a journaling series, wrote the following piece for her body-dialogue.

> **Monica grabs the pen and begins to jot down words that are coming into my head. Monica is my right hand, and she has her own personality. She's strict, a go-getter, loves to experiment, feel, and create. She's demanding, straight forward, and to the point. Lately she's slowly getting more and more rigid. I initially thought it was because I type more than 8 hours a day on a keyboard, but she clearly communicated to me that she's sick of getting bossed around. She's getting tired because she's not creating, just taking direct orders from the brain. Robert, my left hand is very patient,**

and seems to be rather understanding of Monica. Even though, at times, Monica can be quite insensitive and rude. Monica wants to play and lend a hand. She's a healer and she wants to heal. She's upset about the whole situation about the world. She's used to being in a different calmer environment. She just tells me that she's coping with the modern pointless stresses. Robert constantly wants Monica to create new things. She's quite strong, however, there is only so much pain she can take. She wants to build great thing, be inspired, from the heart and not the head, and feel loved.

— By Luz Elizabeth Gudino

Before Luz wrote her piece about Monica and Robert, her hand was hurting her. She was afraid she might be coming down with carpal tunnel. After she wrote the piece giving voice to "Monica," she reported that her hand felt freer.

Lesli, another student, recorded this gentle conversation between her heart and her eyes.

Heart was still
   before sleeping – quiet
after sending out
   so much love that day
It was reflective –
Although love had returned to her
so many times,
   she asked Her eyes –
"Eyes, are you sleeping?"
"My eyelids are closed, but
   I am not sleeping," they replied –
"What is the most beautiful thing
you have seen today?

Was it the mountains? Was it the blue sky?
I felt you were very wide, and made me expand...
    What did you see?"
The eyes opened lazily –
    "The most beautiful thing I saw today
Was other eyes –
    The laughing green eyes of the
shopkeeper selling chocolate
The Baby Blue eyes
    of our husband –
The golden Brown eyes of our son –
    and the Blue green eyes of our daughter
As they laughed
    and looked into our own eyes –
I took in their very spirits –
    And you had to expand
to hold all the love I was seeing –
It was flowing in through me
    and down to you –
And although sunsets
    and sunrises
And mountains
    are also beautiful –
The most Beautiful thing
    I saw today was the eyes of those
    you send love to –"
Heart sighed happily
    and went to sleep

— By Lesli Garnett

Be gentle and playful with this practice, see what gets revealed and enjoy the ride.

Body signals

The body is always giving you signals. Many people speak of getting chills when they feel touched or moved, or when they hear something they perceive as accurate. Other people know things by the fact that their pinky finger wiggles or their right foot gets hot, or their stomach does flips. Ask your body for signals or ask your body to help you develop signals.

You can experiment with finding signals for yourself by asking and then dialoguing with the body in various ways. Find out what the twinge in your gut is signaling, or that uncommon tickle in your throat that comes along once in a blue moon. Maybe it's just an allergy, maybe it's a sign of something to come, maybe it's something you'll never understand but look back on with humor.

Katherine, a participant in a journaling class, wrote about a strange cough that came over her when she went on a first date with someone she met over the internet.

The Cough

When I first moved to Orange County in 2001 I did a lot of internet dating. After all, I had spent the last eight years in Australia and this really seemed like the easiest way to meet people.

For the most part, it worked out fine. My profile was listed on a site called kiss.com – now no longer in service. It's true there were plenty of men on the site I had no interest in kissing, but I had no nightmare experiences – the men I met in person were pretty much who they said they were online. Even though I was awfully selective about choosing the few I would actually meet in person from the pool of hundreds of options online, I had no shortage of dates – usually several dinner or coffee dates each week. In short, it was a great way to become comfortable meeting men again after my long marriage and divorce.

So it was no big deal when I agreed to meet a man from kiss.com for drinks at the Vertical Wine Bar (also no longer there) in Laguna Beach. The man and I had already spoken on the phone a fair amount, and his online profile and picture looked decent enough to make the date list.

The morning of our planned meeting I woke up with an annoying little cough. It wasn't like a cold or infection, and I've never been a smoker, so have never really been a person who coughs. This cough was unlike any I have ever experienced – throughout the day, every time I would open my mouth to speak all that came out was this dry, tickling cough. It wasn't loud, mind you, but it was completely unstoppable. But since I'd never had a cough like this in the past and didn't feel sick, I decided to ignore it and go on my date anyway.

As usual, I hadn't decided what to wear on the date until the very last minute. (The only part of my outfit I did not debate was that I would wear my highest of high heels to see whether this guy would be tall enough for me.) By the time I did my hair, drove to the place, and found a parking spot I was at least 15 minutes late. When I finally got there, I looked around and didn't recognize anyone in the restaurant who looked even remotely like my date's internet photo.

But then I saw this very tall guy standing at the bar looking at me with a big grin on his face –

I don't remember too many details about the rest of our date, but I do know that drinks turned into a long dinner. That in itself would not be all that unusual, but it was quite remarkable under the circumstances – you see, my cough had not gone away.

I could not talk.

At all.

All night, every time I opened my mouth to speak, all that came out was that dry tickly little cough.

So I laughed to cover it up. My date never acted like he noticed – I was amazed that any man could carry on an entire conversation for four hours or so, where the only thing I contributed was a lot of laughter to mask my coughing and a choked out sentence here and there. He must have felt like the funniest man on the planet.

I declined a second date. But accepted a third.

Two and a half years later, we were married. That was five years ago.

I have not coughed since.

—Katherine Ladd

What did the cough mean? Who knows, but Katherine wrote a delightful, well-crafted piece about the body's dialogue system that showed up for that single date, that the class participants all got to enjoy hearing.

The beauty of writing *from the body, about the body* and *through the body* is that it can serve you in several ways. It can give you precious information, enhance your intuition, give you peace, and even assist you in developing skills for a premonitory practice, while also providing source material for stories, poetry, novels, music and song. It can help you to find your character's voice, patterns of speech, rhythm of movement, obstacles hurdled, and direction for their dreams – as well as your own! Such is the brilliance of your work and play with the word.

Questions for your wisdom body

Describe a time when you discovered something *through* your body.

Describe a time when your body absolutely *knew* something better than you or when it told you something you hadn't previously known.

Can you recall a time when you felt a gut feeling of excitement or a soaring in your heart and chest urging you towards greatness you might have ordinarily resisted?

Can you recall a time when your body saved you from a potential disaster? It could have been your dream body that told you something in the night that was of a prescient nature. Or simply a tired feeling that called you to rest instead of driving to the store in rush-hour traffic.

Reread David and Lisa in the previous chapter and scan your life for moments when your body knew something and told you so. It could have come to you through a feeling, subtle as a gnawing discomfort or soft as a tickle of delight.

Recognition of body signals is a practice. When fine-tuned it potentially becomes easier to be aware of what's coming down the pike, in an intuitive way. Body can be likened to a radio signal, an instrument of the Soul that says, "Big boulder coming in the road, watch out, curve around, climb over, or move through." Or "Eat well and rest," or "Get up and move!"

When you write about the *body's signals* you strengthen and clarify your awareness and understanding of them. You embrace *how your body* connects to your heart and gut, to your mind and soul, and to that of the world. As well as how your soul-heart-mind-gut and the world connect and signal back to your body.

The Five-Element Body

Your body is composed of five elements: Earth, Water, Fire, Air, and Ether or Space. These five elements also make up the composition of the planet. Ash is the result when the body is cremated, and ash is part of the element earth.

The body is said to be 70 + percent water. Without it, you die. Add up tears, sweat, blood, urine, digestive juices, soft tissue, the water involved with intracellular activity and a host of other functions, and you find the water element swimming in the body.

In the belly lies fire digesting your foods, not to mention your own personal heating and cooling system that keeps you at a fairly even temperature throughout the days of your life. Your heart and lungs monitor the air and oxygen breathed, and between every cell and pore and fiber of your being there is space, imperceptible, but there, nevertheless.

The relationship of the five elements, and the variation in balance of these elements in your body, determine your health in the same way that the balances of these elements on Earth determine the health of our planet.

The five elements, earth-air-fire-water-space, *live* in your body and govern the body. More than inhabiting the makeup of the body, they are living forces on their own. The Sanskrit word for them is Panchabhuta. Recognizing and honoring the five elements or the Panchabhutas is a mighty practice that increases your understanding of them and strengthens your relationship to them. There is power in this understanding and relationship.

Practice: The elements I

Choose one of the five elements and investigate it. For example if you chose air, make a list of all the associations you have with air.

Air

» Flight
» Planes
» Breath
» Light
» Oxygen
» Heart and lungs
» Pollution
» Flatulence
» Water
» Up
» Sky

Do the same with each element.

Practice: The elements II

Choose parts of your life or memories and associate them with the elements. For example –

> »   Swimming as a child in the lakes – Water
> »   Accidentally lighting a table cloth on fire – Fire
> »   Mountain climbing – Earth
> »   Baby's first breath – Air
> »   Dreams of flying – Ether or Space

Practice: Body dialogue with the five elements

Choose an element, become aware of your physical body's relationship to this element, and track this awareness in your journal.

For example if you choose air, begin with your immediate sensorial understanding of air. You might begin writing about your own breathing cycle, or how the air feels against your bare skin, or the lightness you feel in your body when you skydive or run or dance or sing. Let the feeling of air take you on a journey. Maybe you will be called to travel beyond the body across seas to foreign lands or to other worlds where air is experienced differently. Write in whatever direction you are moved to follow. To complete this writing journey, write your way back to your physical body to find yourself home.

If you choose the element earth, again, begin with the physicality of the body. Ask yourself how it feels sitting in the chair or how the dust or cool floor feels under your feet. If you choose fire, you may recall how the body feels in the presence of heat or in the warmth of the sun. You can do the same with water and space. Always begin by noticing what graces the immediate environment around you and then let the elements take you on a ride. Your observation acknowledges and honors the five elements.

Record what you witness during the week in regard to the elements and your life: Cooking, swimming, bathing, the spaciousness or lack of space in your home, the temperature of the air, the wind.

Focus on one element per day and dialogue with it. Or choose one element to focus on for an entire week. Play with assigning different parts of your life to an element or combination of elements, or assign elements to different parts of your life. Observe what elements show up and predominate in any one given day or hour.

Is there more earth in your life during a single week? More air or fire, water or space? There is no right or wrong in what you discover. This practice is not meant to carve out meaning about anything in your life. It is meant as a joyful and playful practice to explore and hone your awareness of the elements. Use that awareness however it best serves you and your world.

Below is a short writing that lightly incorporates the element water.

Example

I went for a swim this morning, unusual as I usually relegate any exercise routine to later in the day, but I got up and instead of sitting at my desk I swam across the chlorine blue. It was a wise move for my body was happy. I'm most comfortable in water. It's like a second home. I focused my gaze straight ahead neither left nor right, a practice I experiment with from time to time. And then peace of mind floated across my watery screen and I began to ask myself about this peace of mind, first noticing where I don't have it, and then wondering how it would feel to have it. Peace of mind. Peace of mind. I imagined I had peace of mind.

Even now as I type the memory of that experience and watch the little cursor move across the page I stop to close my eyes and imagine peace of mind. What happens? I immediately drop into my body. Ah, yes, the body is safe. It's as if my cells fill out and expand. Shoulders drop and breath deepens. There is no figuring out of any situation, no planning the future, no explaining the past. There is the sound of the dryer and clothes knocking around it. The mrutyunjaya chant plays softly in the background...

Water predominates and splashes in the above piece with "chlorine blue ... most comfortable in water ... floated across my watery screen ... cells fill out and expand." There is a meandering, floating quality to the writing as the words free-associate and the topic moves and shifts in a fluid way.

Observing how the elements show up in your life is a practice that enhances your awareness. Notice how many times in a week weather, landscape, and scenery is described in the news, in books and in films. Notice the sensorial language of the elements such as warm, fiery, fluid, light, airy, hard, or smooth.

When you interact with the elements and saturate your writing with them you add richness, depth and specificity to your words. You create clear pictures for your audience, be they readers, listeners, or business patrons.

You can even play with organizing chapters in a book around the elements.

For example:

Candle Light − Firelight − Sunlight − Moonlight
My Light − Eternal Light − The Light in Your Eyes

Puddle – Rain – River – Ocean – Womb

Fire Chief – Fire Truck – Fire Hose – House on Fire
– Embers Burn – Phoenix Rises – Hearth Restored

Crystal Lake – Emerald Sky – Garnet Hill – Jade
Mountain – Obsidian Cave

You can ascribe elements to people, their names, animals, places, situations, and even to sound. For example: *Granite was a man with limbs the size of a tree. He stood over seven-foot-four, solid like rock, with a voice that had the gravely rumble of thunder pouring from the sky.*

Finally, your recognition of the elements heightens your sensitivities. You start to feel the air against your skin and how the light changes in the sky as storms approach. You read the waters. You feel how the earth moves or sits beneath your feet. You begin to recognize the weather patterns in your own life – including the metaphorical weather *of* life. Something just hits you, a tingle and breath of air, the way light pours through the morning curtains. In stillness, aware of the elements and your relationship to them, you grow another vine for your inner knowing to branch out on. Your creativity and well-being are enhanced.

Practice: Elemental vignettes

» Write a letter from an element to yourself.

» Dialogue with the element.

» Cluster an element.*

» Describe the element using as many of your senses as possible.

» How does the element feel, what is the sound of its voice?

» How does it smell, does it have texture against your skin?

Pen a poem or write a short vignette – and have fun!

---

* For an explanation on clustering, see Appendix I.

Practice: Mixing it up

Choose an element.

Draw on something from your ancestral family or lineage:

» A well-liked food
» A childhood smell
» Something your parents told you about your birth or name
» An antique hidden in the closet

Take something from the world-at-large be it from:

» Your own family
» Your extended family
» Your community, your school, the political world
» From the planets and stars

Choose something that is being addressed or not addressed:

» The environment
» Homelessness
» A new orphanage
» Hiring policies
» A secret or the metaphorical elephant standing mid-room.

Choose something from your life that you observe or that reoccurs:

» A cherished dream
» A grief
» A hurdle you're jumping through
» Something you are excited about
» A heart's desire

Begin and end your journal writing with the element you chose.

When you choose to connect and relate *seemingly* disparate situations, lines of thinking and different views, you come up with interesting and entertaining storylines.

Body wisdom: Body of Earth

By writing you bring attention, body and soul, to the collaborative design of the five elements that work to assist you in your life. From this collaborative design you can discover direction for enhancing your Creative Spirit.

When did the body of Earth tell you something you hadn't previously known? Maybe it was one of the elements in combination with another species, like in the last chapter when the little winged bird got stuck in the sticks by my gate. The veracity of that occurrence was what finally prompted me to follow my dream and fly to Copper Mountain in Colorado.

Recall a time when the body of the earth and one of the five elements – the ocean waters, a volcano, a young arbor, a rock or stone, the earth, air, fire, water, or ether – whispered or shouted something just for you.

The following passages celebrate our connection to the earth, the elements and to each other.

> **We sing the Earth's joy and celebrate our insepa-
> rable and symbiotic relations with the body of the
> Earth by recognizing our life intertwined with the
> oceans, the trees, the mountains and air, with each
> species, and each other. Tasting on our lips the salt
> ocean air, we stand to see birds nesting; we feel
> their flight as wind drifts across our skin. And we
> remember the ancient wisdoms that always have
> been and always will be spiraling through our lives,
> linking one to another as thread woven through
> cloth: individuality within family, family within
> community, community within humanity, and
> finally humanity upon the Earth. For we are made
> from the elements of the Earth, and the Earth is**

made from us. She is made from our ash and from our blood, and she in return remains our hearth.

As we treat ourselves with joy and compassion, so may we come to treat the Earth. And as we treat the Earth with joy and compassion, so may we learn to treat ourselves. Released then, from the fear that has driven us into closets of inaction, released from the powerlessness that has paralyzed our individual lives, and that has placed our increasingly fragile Earth on the endangered species list, we will no longer have to reach out of ourselves to find Source or God. We will know God. We will not have to conquer other nations. We will live in peace with other nations. Making room for our life's breath and our life's spirit to enter into our bodies, we will re-orient ourselves in the flesh, on the earth in a global community. Then, perhaps, deep in our souls, deep in our skins we will find a joy and a peace that passes all understanding.*

Writing about your relationship to earth and the elements sharpens your intuition. Like prescient animals moving to higher ground, protecting themselves from turbulent weather coming their way, your knowledge of earth and body signals can condition you to be alert for what is coming into your life. Your intuition then unfolds to you new directions. In service it whispers, "This way, keep going this way."

---

* From the afterword to *Women Celebrate: The Gift in Every Moment*, compiled and edited by Elizabeth Welles

Five-Element Meditation

Breathe in and relax and as you exhale, exhale breath all the way to the bottom of your breath, and relax again.

As you continue to breathe in and breathe out, let your body soften. Relax your shoulders, your neck and head. And begin to feel into your body just as it is in space right now. Scan the body for any tension, and for places of relaxation and feelings of peace. Notice without doing anything. Notice the body breathing in. Notice the body breathing out.

Now bring your attention to your body and how it is sitting or lying down. Bring your attention to your body's connection to earth. Feel the weight and strength and solidity of your body like a rock or a tree. Recognize and honor the earth element that lives inside your body, the earth element called *prithvi*.

Let yourself scan the earth as if you could fly over the planet. Witness the great natural monuments and megaliths of rock and stones, and witness, too, the small precious treasures of gems that lie still deep in the earth's body. See the green grass and rolling hills of the Earth Mother and honor the earth inside of you. The earth element of your body, borrowed for a time and impermanent, is born from the atomic earth and the energy of Earth. Breathe in this eternal presence of Earth, and as you breathe out relax. Knowing how earth changes and revolves and moves and merges and submerges into water.

Amrita, Jal. Breathe in and relax. Scan and feel your body in space and recognize its fluid nature, your ability to move with grace. Feel into your cells that are supported by water, all the functions of body that use water, the fact that body is seventy percent, or more, water. Breathe in and out and let yourself become fluid. Float as if in a womb of water, amrita, golden liquid ambrosia, and then look out and see the waters of ocean and rivers and streams, the water you drink and excrete. Water can be solid like earth when formed into ice and water can be light as air when evaporated into clouds and then returned as rain. Water in your body, and in and on the earth, water we borrow for a time. Honor water knowing that while it is impermanent in the body, that the energy of water is eternal. Feel the water in your body as one body of water. Breathe in and relax letting the water element dissolve.

Fire, *Agni*, fire in the belly. Center in your solar plexus and breathe in and breathe out and relax, feeling the fires of your digestive power. And so, too, feeling the infinite rays of sun that are born in and of you through the Central Sun. There are suns more powerful than anything of earth, the Celestial Sun, the sun behind the sun inborn through you in your solar plexus. Your solar plexus is your personal solar center. Feel the sun strong in this center and then feel its light spread through your body knowing the spark of Light that you are.

And, so, too, recognize the fiery nature of earth with her volcanoes as well as the fires of the heavens and of the stars, the fires that we create with match and wood, the fire in our stoves and hearths. Breathe in and relax and let this fire element that we borrow for a time, rise and crackle and move into air.

Air, Vayu. Breathe in and know you are breathing air and as you breathe out know the air is breathing you. You breathe air and air breathes you, a symbiotic relation between lungs and body and air, and between air and body and lungs. Feel your body in space and celebrate the lightness of air moving about and around your body. Celebrate in your body the moving and flowing gift of new breath and life. With your deep inhalation give honor to air, air in you, air in sky and of earth, and to all species who use air to fly and glide on this element of lightness. Feel yourself drift and glide and let air dissolve and merge and move you to ether.

Ether, *Akasha*. Where sound lives, the only element that is ever eternal with no relative impermanence, ether and sound, however and whatever you perceive this to be. Be still in the current of ether and sound. Feeling your oneness with this eternity, breathing in and out. Feel sound and expansive space breathing between each and every cell, fiber, pore, atom and molecule of your being … and relax.

Imagine a moon in or around your head, in your third eye or above your crown, a glowing moon in the dark of night. Breathe in and relax. Feel this moon expand and rise. Feel it turning and revolving into the sun with the lightness and brightness of a thousand stars. Radiant and luminous Light pours through the top of your head. Illuminating Light moves through your crown, pouring in and through your body, merging, floating, melting, growing brighter and brighter.

Soften and relax your body even more as you witness the elements of ether and sound, air and fire, water and earth, *akasha, vayu, agni, amrita* and *prutvi*. As your own awareness and reverence for them grows inside of the body and outside the body and in every body, know the body of air, the body of fire and earth and water, ether and sound are alive.

Breathe in and relax and rest. Breathe in slowly and deeply and scan the body. Recognize and move through the elements of the body and of earth. Bring the illuminating Light to any area of your body that wants attention, increased energy or healing love. Take this time to relax giving reverence to the elements and the eternal Light that lives in you.

Soften and feel yourself in space again. Soften your shoulders and your head and your throat and your heart, your belly and your hips, your arms and your legs. Feel yourself in space, feel the ground beneath you, listen for any sounds around you. Become fully cognizant of your surroundings and of your body in your surroundings, and then slowly open your eyes.

Breathe in and soften. Take your pen and write – or just be still.

When Emotional Challenges Become Story-Wisdoms

Fear, grief, fury are powerful emotions that can be witnessed and observed, felt and understood, as information. They can be potent movers and partners in your life that spark right action. Strong surging emotions have even birthed movements towards freedom and peace. Emotions can signal that it is time to find solitude to heal or be in nature, or color and paint or dance and sing. They can help you discern where your energy output belongs, when too much is going out or not enough. They can determine when you need rest to sit and be still or when you need to act. What emotions mean, how they show up, and how you work or play with them is as individual as snowflakes that fall. Additionally, they can provide source material for characters that emerge in novels, subjects in poems and song. You, too, can dance with these informative emotions and transform them to be a force for your good.

Transformation means to change form. And every time you write, you do that. You change the form from what you experience abstractly in your head to what you see on paper. When there is something specific you'd deliberately like to transform in your life, writing it down stirs the transformational process. In seeing what you've written you become witness to yourself. Compassionate witnessing is the beginning for change.

Speaking your words aloud to yourself or another offers you further clarity about the direction of this transformation, even if that direction is not yet apparent. The very act of writing and then speaking, or *sounding* your words, resonates and vibrates your body. The resonance of your own personal rhythm, language, and sound becomes like a prayer to your own self. You now see *and hear* what you long to transform. Then, if you want, you can use your kinesthetic sense to quite literally dance and move with this change. Through writing, seeing, hearing, and moving you set up the conditions in yourself to welcome change. You become receptive to the process. You have sent out the invitation to allow transformation to occur in its own time.

Taking this a step further, challenges, personal or global, can become story-wisdoms. Conversely, you can make up stories by creatively addressing challenges. The story becomes the container, a safe and sacred place in which to transform your world. Social activists do this all the time. They have a *vision* or *story*, a way they would like to see the world transformed and they create this vision for the world to see. A good example of this is Dr. Martin Luther King Jr.'s speech, "I Have a Dream."

Practice: Transformation stories

Write down what, if anything, you might like to transform that is of a personal nature. You can even give it a time frame. For example: In six months I'd like to transform my work situation.

»   I'd like to transform my confusion to clarity.
»   I'd like to hear my intuition more clearly.
»   I'd like to be free from worry and expect a miracle every day.
»   I'd like to come into a place of confidence, rest and surrender.
»   I'd like to transform my relationship with my boyfriend.
»   I'd like to make my home into a center for healing and peace.
»   I'd like to change my yard into a brilliant flower garden.

And write the story of transformation, successful change and completion.

Cynthia the Perfect Owl was a story written as an example for a group of women I worked with in New York City. It is about an owl with a streak of perfectionism that metaphorically clipped her wings. The story reveals how perfectionism emerged and grew into acceptance and wisdom.

Cynthia the Perfect Owl

Cynthia was the perfect owl. Her "whoo" was so singular in its sound that all the animals knew when Cynthia was around. When the animals that could become food for Cynthia, like Mr. Rat and Mr. Mouse, heard her they'd run away and hide. As a result, Cynthia caught little food.

She grew skinnier and skinnier. Her feathers paled and became like dishrags hanging in the wind. Her claws became brittle and dry. She relied on friends and neighbors to bring her left over food, a bone with leftover meat or a plucked eye. Nothing ever too rich or delicious, like leg of rat or breast of mouse. Even Cynthia's eyesight grew dim – night blindness, an owl's worst fate, because she was so deficient in her vitamin intake.

Cynthia practiced changing her whoo whoo's to a less noble kind of sound, but nothing else came out of her. Her whoo whoo's were just too perfect, and Cynthia liked that. She had always wanted to do her best, to prove her best to herself, family and friends. But her expectations for herself were so high that she couldn't even come close by to them. Yet she was determined to change her ways so she could find food. Night and day she called, Whoo, whoo. Whoo, whoo. But it all sounded the same. She became so disenchanted that she flew down to her favorite river, and comforted by the sound of lapping water, sat and wept the whole night through.

Boo whoo, whoo. Boo whoo, whoo.

The next morning, before the sun rose in the sky, when there wasn't a peep of sound anywhere, Cynthia, tired and desperate with her last bit of strength, flew up and up across to the other side of the river – a place of solitude where she would be utterly alone. As she flew, she looked down and saw an owl head in the water's calm reflection. Her head was small, *and* wise. Yes, it was hers! Her feathers ratted and frayed. Her claws were fragile and worn. Well, she was nearly half starved and she had wept the whole night through. But still the sight of her own owl body surprised Cynthia and with a howl and a whoo, she called out an AH! Now, no owl ever made that sound before. She called again, AHOO, AHOO, and then finally, Whoo, whoo. It was the same owl sound but it had a different inflection, stronger emphasis, softer tone. It sounded angelic and light. On the other side of the river, she sat and practiced her new sound – not so perfect, but just right.

As she practiced, no small animal knew it was she, and so Mr. Mouse and Mr. Rat ran by the river's edge and Cynthia swooped down on them and ate them whole – leg, breast and head.

Mm, mm, whoo, whoo. Mm, mm whoo, whoo. I like food in my belly, Cynthia thought.

Over the next few weeks, Cynthia caught more food on her own as her night vision returned. With her new feathers, shiny and fluffed, she flew high in the sky where she saw far and wide, and then swooped down to the earth's floor. She became known as the wisest owl in the land. And in the coming years she knew she was wise too, but she didn't have to prove it or have the perfect whoo.

Practice: Animal stories

Choose an animal to embody a quality you'd like to transform in yourself. For example fear into courage, judgment into acceptance, perfectionism into wisdom, hate into love. Begin writing how your animal would change from being an ornery old coot to a gentle kind aquatic bird that flies with wings of grace. Or how a painfully insecure goose might become a confidant leader of the pack. Or an unfocused tail-chasing dog might become a loyal servant to his creative endeavor of herding sheep. Most importantly, have fun!

Monologues

Writing and performing monologues are great ways to mix and match fiction and fact to create marvelous tales. The following is a monologue I wrote after I attempted to pray for Tom Smith's soul. (His name and details have been changed.) I found I couldn't pray for him until after I wrote this monologue. Only after I had my anger, then found humor in my anger, then moved beyond my anger, was I able to sincerely pray for him and the entire situation. The way was through story.

The Irascible Prayer

Okay, Tom Smith, I'm going to pray for your peace. Let's see, you've been gone almost a month? Okay I suppose I should be waiting or praying through the first forty days, the Buddhist's Bardo. Waiting before I have a real talk with you. I suppose you're resting, but I just want to say Wake Up! You left a lot of people in a real pickle. You left four children. You left your daughter to find you. You left a whole lot of people in a mess, mom and pop-shops, investments and people's life savings. You left my seventy-five year-old mom in a frightful place. So I'm praying for your soul because I want you to have peace so you can get up and get your cronies in Heaven, your CFO angels, the Board of CEO directors and Heavenly Fathers to fix this thing down here on Earth. Yes, I'm doing this for a selfish reason because I want my mom to be okay, and I know there are other investors and so I want things to be okay for them, too. You really hurt a lot of people when you took your life. You think you were hurting then, now how much more are you hurting that you can see

what you've done and how many you've effected. I
don't mean to put any blame or guilt on you, just fix
it and fix it now. Then you can rest in peace okay?
Okay. We got this straight, okay. And I will continue
praying for your soul. I really want to say *your sorry
soul*, but praying for your soul nonetheless or haunting you depending on what happens down here on
earth. You got that? You see it works two ways. We
think down on earth we're haunted. No, that's not
strictly the case. You see we can haunt you, too. So,
no, you can't rest. You can rest just enough to see
this mess and then start praying it up in Heaven
that it's all rectified on Earth, no Chapter 7 for you.
Got that? You don't get off that easy. You already
took the easy way out by taking your life, so now
you've got to get cracking. So I will pray for you.
May the Father, the Son and the Holy Spirit have
mercy on your soul. Oh, Jesus, except your were
Jewish. Okay may Abraham and Moses guide your
way. Now you want me to say the Kadash!? Okay ....
Yit-gadal v'yit-kadash ... *(she recites the Kadash)*

May God have mercy on your soul. May your
children remember you as a loving devoted
father. May all your investors and their money
and my mom's life savings be restored and may
her home be secured. Amen. And may this all be
resolved in a timely manner, right now. And so
it is, blessed be. Amen. And when this is through
I may even thank you for cleaning it up, and
then, then you can rest in peace. Damn it, it's
really hard to pray for you, Tom Smith. Amen.

After I finished this, I was sincerely able to pray for the man's soul and his family. I prayed that the Divine would shed light on the insanity and rectify and restore what people fear had been lost. I prayed for an antidote to fear, which is love. I prayed for peace.

Is something bothering you? Try writing a monologue about it by putting an amusing or mischievous spin on it.

Rekindle your sense of freedom.
Mold material into spiritual reality.
Transform one substance into another.
Transmute fiber into cloth, clay into vessel, stone into crystal,
memory into image, feeling into movement, wind into song,
blood into milk, egg into child, body into worship.

—Meinrad Craighead

Writing Prayer and Meditation

In every spiritual tradition there is reverence paid to *The Word*, and so it seemed fitting to include a section on prayer and meditation in this book. However for some, the word prayer is a trigger with unpleasant memories or of a strict religious upbringing left far behind. But here prayer is addressed not in the religious sense, but as a way to deepen into the quiet and explore your own heart, what it needs to hear, and how it hears it. Even secular scientists find solitude and time to contemplate their theories and to ask, seek or know, and reflect on the wisdom of the ancients.

The very act of writing and then reading aloud to hear your own voice and words, or to let others hear your voice and words, drops you into a listening, reflective-contemplative mode wherein you are received, first by your Self and then another. You will see that you are not alone in suffering and that your words can bring wisdom, solace or counsel to another. Reading your words aloud *and listening into the silence that follows* can unearth revelatory insights for your life and its direction. Finally you will find nourishment to *just be*, able to return to your activities rested and restored.

If you are writing about a challenging situation, then apply your own prayerful words of that still small voice as a healing balm by using *The Voice of Compassion*. If your words are of elation and celebration, then share your understandings and rise of communion and bliss. Celebration is just as much needed in the world and your voice will be appreciated.

You can always return to the basic journaling practices to describe the immediate present moment, slipping between the spaces of time to touch into an ongoing spiritual rhythm that underlies all life. For extraordinary mystical states are available to you right now. Millions of Divine Beings are on the head of every pin, attached to every atom, only waiting for you to turn your attention to them. The essence of life, strands of DNA, molecular structure, and energy in every form that pervades this universe are miracles in themselves. All life is.

You can pen words of prayer, poems, psalm and songs for yourself or to share with others, prayer as self-revelation. Prayers that help you deepen and see what you would love, pursuant of your dreams. Prayer can have a place in your plays, films, monologues and dialogues.

You can create characters of wisdom endowed with the gift of words and prayer at their fingertips. Muses, fairies, elemental Devas, angels, and invisible time travelers with the ability to appear and disappear, get small or large in size, or disguised as humans, can find homes in your stories or act as guide, mentor and friend to you in times of need. Such is the healing power of using your own words as prayer.

Many people think of prayer as a formal way of talking to God, often with getting on your knees. Prayer can be that. But the beauty of prayer – or of simple good thought – is that you can do it in *any* moment, anywhere, with a few words of silence held in your heart. For prayer is simply a way to connect, to deepen faith, and come into the silence.

Connection is a way to hear and be heard, a way to see and be seen. It's a way to acknowledge and validate your experience or that of another. Prayer is the telephone line between you and your own heart and peace. It's the toll-free 1-800 number between you and something 'greater' be that connection to Spirit, God, Source as you define it, or your very own Self. It can be your connection to a noble cause or to an element of nature like the strength of a tree, the ocean, or mountain-sky.

Faith is trust in the *Grace of the Unknown*, a trusting that everything will work out, a trust in love, and a trust in your own Self.

And finally, prayer is an invitation into the silence.

In meditation you dive deeper in silence. In that dive you may initially encounter the body, including sensation and feelings, the noise of your own thoughts or the honking horn outside. But slowly you get to see that although you wear a body and it can be your ally, an instrument of your spirit and soul, you are not your body alone. You are not your feelings, sensations and thoughts, just as you are not the horn honking outside. Meditation is a gentle and open exploration into that which does not change. It is a coming home to the space between what was and what will be, where you are forever in ease. In every moment of reflection, prayer and meditation, there exists the opportunity to move yourself to deeper realms of your own nature with wonder in bliss. Ultimately meditation is your appointment with peace. And as each layer of existence is encountered in silence, it is as if the Magi-Wise is being born.

There are countless kinds of prayers

» Prayers of protection	» Prayers of praise
» Prayers of inspiration	» Prayers of celebration
» Prayers of petition	» Prayers of silence
» Prayers of thanksgiving	» Prayers of peace
» Prayers of communion	» Prayers of healing
» Prayers of silence	» Prayers of blessing
» Prayers of affirmation	» Prayer of loving-kindness

A client once said, "I don't want any more pain in my life. I don't want to suffer in my life anymore." I asked her to rephrase it, "What if you said something like, 'May I be free from suffering. May I be free from pain.'"

Her voice lightened. That one sentence opened up doorways of possibility. I asked her to practice sitting with the phrase. It's not an original. It's a basic Metta or loving-kindness practice from the Buddhist tradition. I asked her to also work with, "May I be free from inner and outer harm. May I be peaceful. May I be peace." This woman, a devout atheist, quietly whispered, "It's like a prayer."

Through prayer and contemplative reflection you create sacred space, which slowly changes your life. When you compose your own meditations and prayers, they hold that much more power and meaning for you.

My mother composed the following prayer for herself that she recites every time she gets in her car to drive:

Prayer for Protection

Surround me with Divine Light
Protect me and my car from any physical harm
And protect all who I meet and pass on the road
Bring me safely to my destination
And return me safely home

What kind of **Prayer or Words of Protection** would you write for yourself or another in need?

What kind of **Prayer or Words of Inspiration** would you write for yourself or for another in need?

One journaling student referred back to the elements to create this Color Prayer.

The Color Prayer

Oh, Creator,
We begin this day celebrating the golden sun,
   and your beauty on this earth.
Bless us with the colors around us –
   Add yellows, pinks and royal purples
To the weavings and threads of our spirits
We are one with you and you are one with us –
   and you shine forth in our eyes
and the sky above us –

Your wind is our breath, and we breathe in your air
   and it fills our lungs with the sky –
And it carries the blood through our veins like the rivers.
Shine! Oh, Sun! In our hearts and in our thoughts –
   May our spirits reflect the spirits of those around us –
May the water from your sky
wash away all negative feelings –
   May the fire from the center of the earth
ignite us to greater purpose –

May your night sky –
   which breaks forth with a kaleidoscope
of colors throughout the day –
Fill us with the Brilliance of the Eternal One –
   and may our lives reflect the colors of these hours –
Our Father, Creator, Ancient One,
   We thank you for our lives
And for letting us live these days on your earth –
   Fill us this day with your Spirit –
We honor you, We praise you –
   We are one with you, as you flow through our lives

Amen –

—Lesli Garnet

Prayers can even be a whimsical celebration of humor and life's absurdities as in the following example, a letter-prayer, written with a light touch:

Hi God, Divine, Great Spirit, Holy of Holies,

Hmm, not sure what to call you these days and not sure you even exist, but just in case, I'm loving you anyway. And if you do exist, you have a great sense of humor. Was out-of-state at a friend's home and went outside on her second-story porch to contemplate your radiant nature just before a national radio interview. Except the glass sliding door closed and locked behind me. Her house is built like a fortress and no one was home so it had to be you. I didn't know you were such a practical joker. I bound over the railing to the staircase and ran down through her neighborhood in bare feet hoping to find a kind soul who could loan me their computer and a phone for the hour, but her block didn't have any kind souls and by the time I found one, it was too late. So I missed the interview.

Canada called the other day. They wanted me to come up to perform and teach and they asked for my non-profit number. Isn't being an individual artist non-profit enough? Only kidding, God, but you get the gist. I, and we (the human race) could use your help. Send a blessing or a miracle or a cure for cancer or juvenile diabetes, would ya? There are a lot of people down here who love you even if they fight over you. We're sometimes a sorry lot but you keep loving us anyway, right? Okay, God, thanks for listening. I'm going to get some chocolate now, and

some tea. And I'll lift my cup high to you and give thanks for the blessings on the way, just in case you're listening. Have a good day God – and God, please keep on watching out for my family and me. Cheers and Love, from one of your skeptics.

Find a prayer

Find a prayer (or song or psalm or poem) you like and ask yourself:

» What do I like about this prayer?
» How does it touch my life?
» How does it effect or strike me?
» How does it relate to my life?
» Guide my life?
» What is this prayer's overarching quality?
» Is it its simplicity? Is it its strength?
» The way the words roll to find a wordless space?
» The way the prayer progresses or moves, its musical nature or rhyme?
» How the language is abstract or concrete?

Write down your answers and then pen a prayer with similar qualities.

Change a prayer

Find a prayer you'd like to experiment with, one you have an affinity for. Read through the original prayer. Then play with rearranging the words and phrases. Or find new words and language that more closely suit your nature and resonate with you. See if you can keep the meaning of the prayer intact while letting it bring you greater peace, solace, or joy. The following is an example using The Lord's Prayer.

The Lord's Prayer

Our Father, Who art in Heaven, hallowed be Thy Name. Thy Kingdom come. Thy Will be done, on Earth, as it is in Heaven. Give us this day our daily bread and forgive us our trespasses as we forgive those who trespass against us; and lead us not into temptation, but deliver us from evil. For Thine is the Kingdom, the Power and the Glory forever and ever. Amen.

Experiment

Gracious Divine of All that is, hallowed are Your Names. Thy Kingdom come; Thy Will be done on Earth and in Heaven, everywhere. Give us this day our daily bread and all that nourishes, serves and protects the Light within. Release us from debt, and all ill will, as we release those who have held them against us. Keep us away from danger and harm, and deliver us to the Light beyond all Light, the Love beyond all Love, and the Peace beyond all Peace. For Thine is the Kingdom, the Power and the Glory forever and ever. Amen.

Simple recipe for prayer writing

» Recognition and Calling Out to the Divine or Connecting Presence

» Expressing and Praising – Asking or Petition, Celebration, Blessing or Affirmation.

» Close with Thanksgiving, Gratitude and Release, knowing you have been heard.

Return to your Sankalpa

Write a prayer for your Sankalpa or for something you wish to transform. Create for your Sankalpa, or for what you are transforming, a prayer of petition or gratitude, a prayer of affirmation or song, a blessing or psalm.

Create a prayer character

Go to your place of unspeakable beauty or into the inner recesses of your imagination. Listen for a wizened prayer friend who speaks to you of the eternal rhythms in nature, the harmony that causes the world to spin and stop, the simple notes in your day. Let your prayer characters bounce and speak, skip or sing, and listen to what they have to say.

> *And this our life, exempt from public haunt,*
> *finds tongues in trees, books in the running brooks,*
> *Sermons in stones, and good in everything.*
> — William Shakespeare

Contemplative practice:
A walk with nature

Take a walk in nature this week. If you are in a snow-cold climate, and being outside isn't an option, then sit by a window and observe. Write down what you see and witness in the natural world.

Then close your eyes and listen to what you hear in the natural world or to what you imagine hearing whether it is birds or the crunch of snow or rain. Listen to what you hear through your body, as in the feel of sun on your skin.

Then drop into your heart, whatever and wherever you perceive that to be, and sit quietly. Is there anything your heart speaks to you?

Then bring in another person or being you feel unconditionally loved by. You may even wish to call back your voice of compassion or spirit of peace. Begin to talk or silently express, to whomever you have called, whatever is in your heart. When you are done speaking what is in your heart, sit in silence. Then listen for what that still small voice has to say back to you. Then sit quietly in silence again. If you feel the urge to speak again, then do so – and listen again. When you feel complete, open your eyes and look around the room and feel the Presence from where you sit. Then take your pen and write. You may even choose to write with your eyes closed! When you are done, put the pen down and sit still in your heart, feeling the embrace of the natural world.

You have been in communion with nature and with your own heart. You have been witnessed by another being and finally you have acknowledged your own wisdom by writing.

Additional qualities to contemplate and write on:

»	Appreciation	»	Love	»	Celebration
»	Wisdom	»	Hope	»	Compassion
»	Peace	»	Quiet	»	Harmony
»	Beauty	»	Silence	»	Joy

Prayer, meditation and reflection can inspire the impetus to connect and create. Just as creativity can inspire a hushed awe that silently nourishes the heart and soul. It is a never-ending dance.

The prayer of being prayed

There are times when it is as if we are not praying but are active participants in an orchestration of prayer. When it is as if the land, the earth, the sun and sky are *praying for us* or *praying us*. Times when words, ineffective, don't come, have no meaning, and are lost. As if the beat of our own hearts are too loud. Such a time occurred when I traveled in India.

Badrinath is the Vishnu Temple, the second temple we visit. Terrorists have threatened it, since it is considered one of the most holy temple sights in all of India. So at the entrance to the town, the men are ordered off the bus and searched by machine gun carrying young soldiers. The women are searched on the bus. We pass inspection and are allowed through the gateway into paradise. In Badrinath, I feel like I'm walking in the time of Christ. Holiness pervades the air. Steamy mist rises from burning hot sulfur springs, where we take our wash for purification and refreshment before going to the temple. Beggars line the bridge across the water, and there is an increasingly loud, carousing pace as we approach the temple. Everyone in bare feet on cold stone, the air charged, singing, dancing, chanting. Yet I hear nothing. I'm aware of all that is happening, but it is silent. I move and walk, walking as if in a stupor, I don't stumble. There is a market full, a temple full of people, and I am mystified because with all the noise, nothing bothers me. Amidst absolute craziness, I am peace. Amidst miles of clatter and chatter, I want nothing. Prayer is even too loud. It already floats thick in the air

**like clouds that sit on these mountaintops, like
silent emperors forever at hand, commanding
while doing nothing. And the earth is praying
me, the sky, the water, the wind. I understand
only with heart, feet, breath, gut, and senses that
touch and taste, smell and hear, to remember
something ancient, real, vast. Nothing can take
away this peace, and I am one with whatever is.**

Can you recall, or invoke now, the peace where you are being prayed
by Peace? Have you ever felt like you were part of an orchestration
that loomed larger than life?

Imagine …

        Remember …

                Invoke …

                        Write …

A Story-Sound, Space-Prayer Movement Meditation

Space and spaciousness are ever present, but the daily grind we often find ourselves in can bring us into a more contracted feeling-state. The good news is that our bodies are designed as fluid mobiles, as we are mostly made from water. Therefore we can easily reverse contraction through simple observation, sound, and prayerful movement.

By opening and embodying the space in and around you with movement and sound, new designs, ideas and story-gems are more likely to emerge. It is one way — through the wave of listening to the story-sound and space-prayer.

Find a prayer or create a prayer, or simply find a series of sounds that you love. This can be a mantra or hymn you already know. Stand and begin to quietly speak or sing the words aloud as you feel the space around you. Take notice of the quality of air and light, moisture, dryness, shadow or sun. Begin to add movement to this space-field you deliberately create, witness, and enter into. Let your movements be very slow. Exaggerate your movements. Touch your body as if opening the pores and space between your skin, your tissues, your cells, and the very atoms of your being. Reach up and down and sideways. Make arcs and circular movements. Walk slowly around while you speak, sing or chant.

Feel free to engage a practice you may already have, like Tai Chi or Yoga. Add a prayer like The Lord's Prayer or the Gayatri Mantra, incorporating the words and seed sounds into your routine. Feel free to create new sounds by toning with your voice.* Experiment and play

---

* For more information on toning, refer to the book, *Toning: The Creative Power of the Voice*, by Elizabeth Laurel Keyes, published by DeVorss Publications.

with this easy flow of movement, sound, language and voice.

By calling on your voice and body, and the space you inhabit, you shift your awareness. You cross thresholds and expand your sense of spaciousness from where creativity naturally flows. Continue this meditation for at least ten-minutes. Then listen to how your body feels. Listen to the sounds in and around you, to where thoughts and feelings are focused. Listen into the stillness and the wisdom of your breath.

When you feel inspired, take a pen and paper and begin to write whatever comes to you to write about. Let your writing be spacious and flowing like poetry in motion.

Your Creative Expression

I hesitate to define creativity. Maybe it is better left to poetic metaphor. Define it one certain way and it will expand into something else. This is because creativity is inherently braided with the mystical. Like the mystic or visionary, artists often draw their answers from within; learning and expressing what is within themselves or that which is within interrelated with their world. You can't tame creativity and there are no hard rules and systems that can effectively be relied on all of the time. For creativity is like wild horses that roam and wild trees that grow. Follow your creativity and you're in the unknown, in uncharted regions. However there are familiar fundamentals that can be recognized and appreciated; universals in its application, for creativity acts through all of us in a similar vein. Using the tools of intuition, instinct, and imagination you can move through the doorways of your inner worlds, where the answers to life's questions lay.

The good news about your creativity

Creative energy acts in and through your life. Call it a Force, Divinity, Soul, Universe, or your very Self. It is the same.

Creativity *is* your nature. It is the force in you that is ever expansive.

Your creative expression is unique. Your life and experiences are distinct. How you perceive, feel, think and make connections is specific to you. Your creative process, the way you listen to or follow it, is singular. It is a marriage of forces, you and your world interacting.

Creativity includes your unique expression of that which knows no bounds. Creativity is your original way of discovering, seeing, hearing, expressing and communicating that which you have not seen, heard, expressed or communicated before.

Creativity will ultimately lead you to greater levels of contentment, freedom and peace. When you are involved with your own creative rivers of inspiration your childlike impulses are rediscovered. It is the child-sense, reveling in freedom from inhibition, innate with its open curiosity and ability to play, which provides a gateway into the mystery of life and into the mystery of creativity.

You are gifted with a myriad of creative possibilities, many rivers and many streams. This understanding provides a portal that there are always outlets for your creative quests. There are solutions to answers, mysteries to be embraced, help for quandaries, and missions for your desires. There is joy, beauty, relief and peace in this knowing.

You can learn to harvest the bounty of creativity. There are steps you can take to invite and hone the creative voice to speak, to dance, to play.

The Four Wisdoms of Creativity™

The Four Wisdoms of Creativity™ first knocked on my door when I was moving through a difficult time. They tiptoed in, whispered in the gentlest of ways, and began to redirect my life. The Wisdoms are a branch of *The ISIS Method for Stress Reduction*. The cornerstone premise for the ISIS Method is that when you are involved with your creativity, your stress is reduced. Sometimes in a workshop or retreat I might say, when you are involved with your creativity in a *balanced* way, your stress is reduced. Balance: it's what we so often strive for. However I have to laugh at that. There are times when creativity can look like anything but balance. Creativity is a force of nature. Like the wind it can hurl you up, toss you around, lift you high, and set you down like Dorothy on new ground. But more than being a force of nature, *Creativity is a force of Spirit.* A Spirit that is ultimately benevolent and loving in nature.

The Four Wisdoms of Creativity™ is made up of four simple principles with accompanying practices, a loosely guided treasure map to guide you back to your own creative self. They are not meant to be strategies carved in stone. They are simple offerings and suggestions to help you *re-member* how to *listen* and *commune* with your own heart and soul.

The Four Wisdoms of Creativity™ are:

» Move in the direction of what gives you energy
» Be involved with what you love
» Be receptive
» Do as little as possible

No single wisdom is more or less important than any another. Rather, they operate in unison inviting you to travel the roads that call you to adventure. Whether you ride along easily or tirelessly plow, it is worth the effort. Because in discovering what you love and what gives you energy, you find a way of living that contains both passion and peace.

When we do this collectively the world changes. As we witness this glorious change, we are compelled to acknowledge that although we travel different paths, we are the *same* the world over in our desire to create and enrich our lives. What grace that our unique paths, more varied and infinite than the stars, would lead us to each other in this simple understanding.

When I teach *The Four Wisdoms of Creativity*™, one of the first questions I ask the individuals and group is: What would you love to create? This question helps you to dream and clarify what is ripe for you now, waiting to be born.

To answer this question, begin by creating sacred space and uninterrupted time away from washing the dishes, answering the phone, doing the laundry or taking care of the kids. People have different ways of creating their own quiet. What that is and how that occurs can also change from day to day.

You can light a candle or play your favorite music. If you prefer, take a drive to the beach or the mountains where you can sit alone and write. For some people getting lost in a restaurant with a busy loud patronage and clanging dishes provides the necessary atmosphere for them to move into the center of their quiet selves.

Practice: What would you love to create?

Take a piece of paper and write at the top of your page the question: *What would I love to create?* This question and the words used are specific. You can also write: My Joy List. However the words: *What would I love to create* are chosen for their wondering power. The answer to this question invokes possibility and your positive abilities.

Would is a word of invitation. It is different from *could*. The word *could* is conditional. It has definitive answers associated with it, usually a yes or no. You can always do something but would you want to, choose to, love to? When the word *would* is used in a question it reflects possibility and sometimes vulnerability, openness, which leads to the word love. *Love is the most powerful force in the Universe. And Creativity is born from love.*

You are about to take a personal excavation exploring unknown shores to rediscover what makes you feel good, what brings joy, what gets you going. Take off all bars, open the prison gates, unknot the ties, and move into the imaginary realm where anything is possible. Ask yourself, what dreams, wishes, and desires fill my deepest longings? What would I love to create that brings deep joy, peace, satisfaction, contentment, excitement, or adventure?

You are inciting the play-filled wondering Dreamer, the often forgotten one, yet the one who never forgot you. Write down everything that comes into your stream of consciousness: personally, professionally, creatively, artistically, home and garden, travel, health and relationships. Write down the outrageous – the dreams you'd love to create but don't dare tell anyone about. Dreams you'd love to create but think aren't possible. Dreams you'd love to create but are far away from your present everyday reality. The dreams you'd love to create given that all the conditions in your life are perfect: health, family, financials, and that you had the time and energy, complete permission, and felt free enough. What would you love to create? What would you love to embark on?

The outrageous is encouraged because it is joyful and energizing and because it gets you outside the box of limited thinking. You could not have the thought to do something or take action on it if it were not already in the realm of possibility. What you would love to create does not have to make sense. You don't have to know how it will occur. Sometimes not knowing (or non-knowing as I prefer to say) is more powerful as long as you hold the overall vision or dream. This way it leaves the details malleable. You will plan as you move towards your vision while remaining open to what may come that you cannot yet see. For now, you only have to know that these are the things you *would love to create.*

If you can't think of anything, then begin to recall what you loved as a child. Did you love to play outside and get muddy dancing barefoot in puddles? Did you love to sing to music on the radio? Did you love taking apart your toys and then trying to put them back together again? Did you love to watch the night sky and think about who or what else might be out there?

Fill the page and write some more. Write down qualities you would love to embody more often in your life like humor, joy, security, peace, courage or health.

A composite from several people looked like this:

- » I would love to go back to school and study ceramics
- » I would love to own a children's bookstore
- » I would love to create a healthy and strong body
- » I would love to move out of the city to a country home
- » I would love to move to the city
- » I would love to win the $88,000,000 lottery
- » I would love to create a business designing clothes for kids
- » I would love to work with children in Africa
- » I would love to build sustainable homes for the homeless
- » I would love to travel to Italy and Ireland for six-weeks
- » I would love to create a new car
- » I would love to create someone to clean house once a week
- » I would love to create more time to read
- » I would love to create a joyful significant relationship
- » I would love to create a new wardrobe in all bold colors
- » I would love more laughter and dinner parties in my life
- » I would love to take photos of mountains and have a show
- » I would love time alone in nature.
- » I would love to heal world poverty
- » I would love to work with horses and at-risk children
- » I would love a create a tropical plant garden
- » I would love to get my masters in engineering
- » I would love to have more inner and outer peace
- » I would love to create planets where people live to be a 1000-years old
- » I would love to start a foundation to eradicate world hunger
- » I would love to create a good news television network

Lists are about listening

Lists are about listening. List making sources your originality. You hear and write in a playful way that which engages you creatively. You loosen the hinges on musty thinking that kept your dreams locked in a box. You are breathing life into them and into yourself! With your hand gliding across the page, your breath deepening, listening to quiet music, or none at all, it is as much a kinesthetic experience as any.

A free associative list is the *ask* in *ask and you shall receive*. It's the kind of asking that creates a level of receptivity in you. You forage the gems floating in your subconscious, inviting them to the surface of your conscience. This places *you* on notice, bringing to your attention what it is that you'd really love to create and begin to receive.

List making is a journaling practice that may appear linear but can be anything but linear. Sounds paradoxical? It isn't. Words poured on paper *without restriction* encourages freedom. It is the *feeling* of being free from restriction that opens up to you the world of ideas, words, possibility, and that which you *would love* to create. The free-associative spilling out of what you would love to create must come first lest you leave out something of import and value. The irony is that you will, in all likelihood, discover a *creative logic* but it may not appear in accordance to what you are accustomed to thinking of as organized, logical and orderly. For creativity has its own order and originality apart from what you may traditionally think or would like to impose on it.

The beauty in writing down what you would love to create is that it both focuses and sets free your imagination. You get to see what excites and inspires you. Many times when people do this, things they didn't expect mysteriously pop up. If you're working with a group of people or have a family of friends you are comfortable with, then try this practice with the group and read your lists aloud. You will find yourself inspiring others with your list and being inspired by their lists.

Although I've taught this practice for years, I am still amazed at how good people feel once they're done.

Lists grace refrigerator doors: grocery lists, to-do lists, children's schedules, carpool and school lists. Why not let this creative list also feed you? Tack it on your fridge, by your bed, on an altar or at your desk. Gaze at it, and let the swirl of images and dreams give fire to your passions. This is not to become another to-do list, and if it ever does become that, then toss immediately. In any event, you may one day toss all your lists away. You will have reignited the inner confidence that there is an order to what seems like madness. You will see that everything arrives, disappears, and arrives again in its time. For the Universe offers ample possibilities to create, love and enjoy. It is an endless well.

Alternative paths

If writing a list is not to your liking, there are alternative ways to proceed. Write down what you would love to create as a prayer, a poem or song. Or cluster. *(See Appendix I)* Be creative with this practice. It isn't the technical way in which it is done as to *how you feel* that is important. You can create a collage. Get stacks of old magazines and newspapers, and with scissor, glue and poster board, cut out pictures that move you. *You don't have to know why they move you,* just cut them out and paste them on a poster board. Draw, paint, or use magic markers to create stick figure drawings of what you'd love to create. Or simply ask that one heart's desire present itself above all the rest. That will suffice.

But wait, horror, what if nothing comes? If there is a lack of clarity or you can't think of anything to write down at all or if there is terror or inertia so strong that you feel paralyzed, don't fight it.

Take a moment to feel into those strong feelings, and write them down.

Write down exactly what it is you are feeling, write about anything at all, even about this practice. *This is a stupid practice that makes me feel dumb because I'm 65 years-old and don't know what I want!*

I feel inertia, like a big blob of rock. I feel paralyzed and breathless like there is a choking sensation about my waist.

Dump all the feelings that are keeping you blocked in any way by writing them out. Write the specific details of what you see or hear. *I see lines and squiggles in the wood of this table. They look like dancing bears.* Or observe your surroundings and doodle.

And breathe, breathe, breathe!

If you feel the urge to go for a long walk, then go. When you come back from that walk, do some writing. Write down your observations about the walk, or about your arrival back home. You can't force knowing so just trust that *you know everything you need to know when you need to know it.* There is Grace in the unknown. It is a powerful place to sit. It is a place of trusting that everything is all right in this one moment now. It is the space between what was and what will be, between one thought and the next, between one feeling and the next. It is the place-space of possibility. Trust your Self. Trust your Soul.

What's Soul? I may regret writing this, knowing that it will change and rearrange, but here goes. Soul is a vehicle for the inexplicable force some refer to as God or Self. It is the ever-expansive part of you that is also the eternal witness sailing in and out of time. It makes no differentiation between success and failure, birth and death, war or peace. Soul is both container and sieve. It is the container from where all experience is held as we sail in and out of time. It also holds the blueprint we came to Earth with: to experience, to witness, to know. Yet there is also some sieving process through which the Soul discerns which way to move and fly for Life's unfoldment, not for an individual's unfoldment but for *Life's* unfoldment. And although Soul acts as a clearing-house, possibly arranging *how* we hear and act, thereby moving the individual in a direction that calls, sometimes to the very dismay of that individual, the Soul has no preference for it is the Eternal Witness.

The *Soul is whole* beyond polarity, paradox, judgment or fear. Soul is the boundless part of you, free of all restriction. If I could draw a picture it would be of concentric circles one within the other. In the inner most circle would be imagination, held within the circle of creativity, held within the circle of intuition, then held by the Soul. The Soul would have no circle. It freely interfaces with the Spirit of Beingness. The Spirit of Beingness is who we are and what we live in all the time – if there were really an *in*, but there really isn't an *in* because if there were an *in* then there would be an *out*. And Existence cannot be contained in or out of anything. For Spirit knows no birth or death. It is, we are, eternal and free. Soul inhabits and speaks through the body, however the body does not ever capture the Soul. Creation is about the individual's unique expression of *That* which knows no bounds.

Journaling is one way to engage this sieving process allowing Soul to act as a clearing-house. Playing with paint and image and clay or fiber or movement and story and song does the same thing. But when absolutely nothing comes, you are simply being called to wait. Wait with the remembrance that creativity never goes away; sometimes it just goes underground. All you need is a seed. Trust that every seed you need is already within you.

Listen for the tidbits of inspiration that speak through your nights and days. Watch for the inexplicable synchronicities that swirl through your life. Continue to ask your self, what would you love to create? The seeds for these practices are love, for what you love grows. Be gentle with yourself as gentility is a significant act of love. Water the tiniest of seeds and sprouts will break ground, beckoning you to keep watering.

The Quality Meditation

Come into a place of peace within yourself. Breathe in a long, slow deep breath, and exhale fully releasing all tension, stress and thought. Bring breathe in again and then let your breath soften into an even and natural rhythm for you.

Soften your shoulder, your arms and hands, and relax your face. Soften your mouth and your eyes. Breathe into your heart. Breathe into your throat. Breathe into your belly and your solar plexus. Breathe into your lower abdomen, your pelvic girdle. Breathe into your hips and legs and feet.

Feel your whole body in space, where you are sitting or lying and what you are sitting or lying on. Feel the air around your body, in back and in front of you, and to the sides of you. Breathe.

Peace, center on the quality of peace, and what that feels like or would feel like to you. Feel a sense of peace in your body. It can be anywhere in your body: your heart, your belly, your eyes, your hands, or your toes. Locate one place in the body where you experience peace. Notice the sensation of peace and then slowly expand this feeling of peace through your whole body. Let it spread through every fiber, pore, and cell of your being. Then breathe peace out through your body, through every pore, fiber and cell of your being. Feel, see, or imagine yourself in a bubble of peace or riding in a wave of peace. Feel peace in the air around you, and relax. Soften and relax again.

Stay here for as long as you would like, and rest.

If you choose, allow an image of what you are creating in your life or of what you would love to create to arise. Allow the image to float in your heart, or in any part of your body: your belly or your hands. The image may be a replica of what you are creating or the image may be symbolic. It doesn't matter. Let the image dance and float. An entire vision of life may unfold before you. Maybe a specific vision of something you need that is materially necessary for your life appears, like a new car or a college degree. Or maybe this image is a quiet whispering, a feeling or voice that you hear. A symbolic representation of an unspoken desire for a deeper peace in your heart may appear. You may see or feel nothing at all. That's all right. Many find they are content to sit in the quiet.

If you feel called, you can ask that your imagination call forth a special place in order for you to witness that which you'd love to create: a silken cloth screen in your mind's eye, a field of spring green grass, the vast blue sky. Use your seeing sense, your hearing, feeling and smelling sense and your cross-sensory imaging abilities.

To get an even clearer understanding of this that is being created, ask yourself, are there any additional images that come up? Any sounds in your picture? Any voices? Who is speaking? What time of day is it? What is the temperature? Are you inside or outside? Is there a color or texture you can feel about or around the vision? Is it in your body or outside your body or in the body of nature? Are there elements you associate with it? Does your vision have a voice with which it can talk and what does it say? What does it wish to speak to you about your life right now? Let whatever presents itself float through like a parade of passing images and sensations. Observe in silence whatever graces the space. You may be taken further into the quiet with nothing appearing. And quiet is beautiful and most sufficient, a place of peace and rest from where all creative inspiration is fed.

Now look at the qualities *behind* your creation. For example if you are focused on the need for a new car, and that is what you would love to create, the surge towards this car may lie in the need to have safe transportation. A new car may also mean security, travel, expanding horizons, or even prestige. If you were focused on creating an afternoon daycare center, for example, the qualities behind this may be in the desire to nurture or offer service, or to be in joy and celebration and play with children. Ask yourself what are the qualities behind *your creation* that give you an energy boost, that feed and nurture you right now? Be with those qualities and breathe.

Relax deeply. Relax your eyes and mouth and shoulder and heart. Are there any more symbols or images that are present? Simply register what comes. Like a dream, symbols and images may occur that you do not understand. That is all right. For symbols can bring gifts in the offing; ever deepening expressions available for you to explore if you choose. Relax deeply and invite peace into your vision.

Take a deep breath and relax. Thank yourself and thank the vision, sounds, and energy of what has appeared. Soften your face and eyes and let what has arisen dissolve away, knowing it doesn't go away but instead melts back into you for further development and inner understanding. Return to peace. Breathe peace through every fiber, pore, and cell of your body. Breathe peace. Feel it in your heart, in your solar plexus, in your lower belly. Feel it in your head, and in your throat, in your hands and your feet. Feel peace in and around you.

Take a deep breath in and soften your face, your eyes and mouth. Know that in this moment, this one moment, every thing is all right. Soften into this knowing by relaxing your shoulders, relaxing your whole body and breathing all the way to the bottom of your breath.

Become aware of any sounds around you. Become aware of your fingers and toes. Become aware of your body in space. Become aware of any thoughts you are experiencing, and become aware of the environment around you. Rest and be still for several minutes and when you are ready, open your eyes.

Gently take in the room you are in. Register the feeling of your body. Take a deep breath and relax back into your day.

Peace be still, peace be still.

Stories as the Fiber of Our Lives

*Storytelling is as old as time. Through story, song and dance
we have lived and loved, created community, celebrated
and grieved. We hear and tell them constantly. Stories
make us uniquely human and connect us soul to soul.*

It is as if we are made from the fiber of stories. What are stories?
They're our words and language, our arts and crafts, our paint on
canvas. They are the way we live in our homes, the way we build
and the buildings themselves. Story is the tree whispering its secrets
as its sap rises in the bark. Story is the way we organize and make
sense of what has no sense and what has no organization. Story is
our allowance, our permission to be ourselves at the deepest layer
of existence. Story makes us uniquely human and connects us soul
to soul. Story is a road and a path into the silence, from where more
stories will spin and it is the breath of Life singing to us Her song.

We hear and tell stories constantly but some are transcendent. They
reflect our lives, where we've come from, who we are, where we're

going. They are like the stones of Earth, storytellers themselves with history, solidity and strength. Even if it is the story of inexpressible sorrow told through silence, no words or song. Story, like music, like wind, here and then gone. Like birth and then death, a remembered beating in our hearts. Through story we embrace mystery and experience the mystic in our cells. We experience wisdom that inspires us to new breath and life until we live by the no-breath of spirit alone.

I know the power of stories because I have seen first-hand their mighty strength to lift and lighten perspective to help people grow in a new dimension that restores their faith and appreciation for life's variant colors. I have seen people remember the beauty in their dreams, and be catapulted towards them with fresh inspiration by hearing the story of another who is following their bliss, or by writing their own, and sharing that with another human being.

Journaling is a place to start, the diving board and the drawing board from where you can jump off to discover how your story-words impact and serve.

What stories can do for you

1. Stories give solace to the weary and grieved

Stories lift you above the disappointments and dross.

Even sorrowful or difficult stories whisper that you are not isolated in your pain; there are others who have felt the same.

Stories reduce anxiety and inspire you to think in a different way that relaxes the body.

Conversely, when the body is impacted by story and story-sound, it relaxes hardened and conditioned thought.

2. Stories make you healthier

Stories access the entire body. The resonance of language and music and sound vibrates the body, heart and head. Stories that incorporate sound, color, shape, texture and rhythm when felt, touched, heard and seen wake-up sleepy bodies!

Stories access the entire brain as neural networks connect, reorganize and expand.

Stories enhance memory, concentration, and attention span. Stories heighten your sensory imaging ability. (In other words, your ability to imagine using all your senses, which wakes up parts of your brain!)

Stories support discernment. You are lifted up out of yourself. You get to see yourself in a story – or not see yourself in a story.

3. Stories give meaning to your life

Stories help you explore your deeper wisdoms and life experience.

Stories develop unrealized potentials.

Stories organize your experience.

Stories can help you make sense of what has no sense.

4. Stories create

Stories inspire you to access your imagination and creativity.

Stories stretch the imagination and make the unbelievable believable, the impossible possible, expanding the horizons of what you, too, can create.

Stories inspire confidence, laughter, faith, and enable you to smile at your foibles.

Through story you dare to play, share, enjoy and have fun!

5. Stories celebrate relations to Self, the stars, and others

Stories remind you of your ephemeral and solid nature.

Stories enlarge your sympathies, compassion and understandings.

Stories bring to your heart the common thread of humanity, to celebrate life in all its variant colors.

Stories take you where no one has gone before, into the unknown, and to where Grace lies.

6. Stories inspire you to be the mover, shaker and peacemaker

Stories are a way of exchanging information and ideas that promote dialogue that can enlarge understanding of each other's ways.

Stories enable you to find compassion and respect for yourself and with your fellow beings on the earth.

Stories honor and celebrate differences and similarities.

Stories mobilize you to act.

7. Stories connect you to Source, as you perceive that to be

Stories are how you live and bridge to something larger than yourself, be that a Divine Being, a group cause, or your own heart-centered Creative Self.

Stories are a nurturing source for flourishing survival.

Stories heal and bring you closer to your Divine Self.

Through story you witness, celebrate and are uplifted into the recognition of peace, which is ultimately who you are.

Journaling to create your stories

Journaling allows the creative gems of your inner coffers to find their way to the surface of your life. Your words, stories, poems, and songs will be born and find form.

Journaling to the writer can be likened to the sketchpad for the artist, the blueprints and designs for an engineer or a series of quick studies for a painter. The journal is the playground and the playing ground, an ideal place to let your imagination soar. It is where you can write and flush out your ideas, and where your ideas can then lift-off to take flight into story. Story in any form: visual, dramatic or literary. Even ideas for a business or non-profit can be unfolded through the journal as story. Your journal and story-words can contribute not only to your personal well-being and peace, but also to the well-being and peace of others. Your words can be sprouts of inspiration, gifts and guidance for your family, your friends, and the world-at-large.

How do you create from your journal? Broadly. First get down on paper the big strokes of your direct experience, or your raw and unfiltered ideas.

Then look and see what tickles your fancy. What can you sustain working on for a period of time? Which buds will you pick to replant and grow into story? Which buds will you prune to use elsewhere in later works? And what buds will you leave to die on the vine – or keep growing on the vine till they ripen for plucking? Which buds call after you? Those that won't let you sleep until they are attended to or that keep showing up in your life saying, "It's my time!"

In writing, you will continually hone your work and you will always be making discoveries. At some point you will say, "Done." You have orchestrated your creative symphony. It is time for its birth into the world, and for you to find new creative buds to play with.

The Art in Journaling

> *Tell me a fact and I'll learn.*
> *Tell me a truth and I'll believe.*
> *But tell me a story and it will live in my heart forever.*
>
> — Indian Proverb

Your writing, your life

Everyone is influenced by the world they live in, and our worlds and our lives find their ways into our stories. JK Rowling, author of the *Harry Potter* series, once lived next to a cemetery and in a town where there was a castle. Cemeteries and castles play a significant role in her books. There are a number of key incidents and inspirations from her life that find their way into her work.

The Red Shoes is a cautionary fairy tale by Hans Christian Andersen about the effect of vanity and compulsion. In short, a girl named Karen becomes enamored with a pair of red shoes that take over and ruin her life. Anderson was influenced by an incident he witnessed in childhood. A rich customer sent his father red silk in order for him to make a pair of red dancing slippers for her daughter. His father worked long and hard, even adding his own red leather to the slippers. When the customer saw the shoes, she told him they were trash and that he ruined her silk. His father ripped the shoes apart in front of the customer, saying that he might as well then ruin his leather. Such is the power of witnessing and letting life's events stir in your heart until story abounds.

Fact or fiction

Great stories have been born with a single thread of actual fact intertwined with spools of emotional truths that get catapulted through the story process and emerge full born plays, films, seeds for events from conferences to musical extravaganzas. Truth does not mean it happened, and fact doesn't mean its right. Moral and ethical compasses can be composed of greater Truths that have nothing to do with what factually happened, with this world, or with the rules of society.

One advantage in fiction is that you can write what cannot be heard or said directly when it is fact. This is especially true if the subject matter is raw and stark, or if you have characters with strong, controversial viewpoints. In story things can be said directly because it is just a story, and therefore people are more likely to stay with it without threat. In some cases, story becomes code for the subject matter at hand as opposed to works of fact that can potentially become points of contention. Whether you choose fact or fiction or some combination of the two, when you put emotional truth with common ground to all humanity into story your audience is more apt to listen.

When I was invited to write a monologue about shoes, I had not a clue as to what to write about. I first went to my life to look for material. After combing personal history, an informal interview, and some light research, my imagination took off and the monologue, *In Defense of Feet*, was born.

In Defense of Feet

A barefoot woman walks amidst a sea of shoes

Shoes-feet, feet-shoes. I use to have a lot of
shoes. Exhibit A *(She points to an array of shoes.)*
I didn't know what to do with them, because I
was taught not to throw things out, even though
I felt they were useless and shaped on old
ideals. So yeah, they sat in back of my closet
for a long time as I slowly evaluated the pros
and cons of shoes and feet and learned I was a
lover and connoisseur of the unadorned foot.

I remember the first time I was going to India,
my traveling partner looked at my stuff and said,
"How are you going to travel with all that stuff?"
He made me dump it all out and said, "This has to
go, this has to go, and these definitely have to go!"
(She picks up the imaginary items and then the boots)

"Put that back, put them down! They're my boots,
they're my boots! Don't touch my stuff, don't
touch my stuff!!!" I wanted my boots. I needed
my boots to walk around India in case I wanted
to trek. And my boots were a gift from someone
I didn't even know who had hardly worn them
because they were too small for her feet and so
she gave them to me. "If they fit, they're yours."

Shoes were important for a time and I remember the first time I learned to tie my shoes. I was
six with blue sneakers in Puerto Rico. *(She bends
down to tie her sneakers, trying to tie the imaginary knot over and over again.)* "I DID IT MOM!
I DID IT! I tied my sneaker." And the world of

lace and knots opened. At eight I went to the duck pond with my grandma and I was wearing a pair of white sneakers. Well, I started kicking my feet and singing to myself at the edge of the water just wondering what it would be like to kick my shoes off and be free from them – to see them rise and fall into the pond. And they were loose and so ... *(She sings to herself and kicks her shoes off.)* "Grandma, Grandma, my shoes fell into the pond!!!" Well grandma was a fisherwoman – who got sick on boats – but a good fisherwoman nevertheless. And she said, "That's all right, I'll get my fishing gear out of the trunk and we'll fish them out!" And that she did. And I never knew how smart and well-equipped Grandmas were till then.

I admit, I graduated to heels in high school. And at my prom I wore red high-heeled pumps. I remember my father cracking a joke to my mother, making this little face and saying something about "Ladies of the Night." I wasn't sure what he meant but took it to mean that there was something about my red high-heeled pumps that Ladies of the Night might like!

Red pumps, white and blue sneakers, red white and blue – maybe it's American culture, 'cause I never knew what the big deal was with shoes or why people get foot fetishes. But I do understand the need for shoe health care reform where everyone should have a right to a nice, warm, comfortable fitting pair of shoes where their toes aren't stuffed into a can like sardines. But I didn't understand the shoe fetish that's taken the country by storm with Shoe Pavilion, Shoe Palace, Shoe Heavens!

(For Heaven's sake!) So I did a study and took a
survey and learned that it started with fashion.

First there was Lana Turner when tight sweaters
were all the rave. But then with Gloria Vanderbilt
Jeans, the advent of the ass kicked in, and the sites
of men dropped. This bit of information comes
directly from my family friend, Mike. But what
gets me is that I don't get being uncomfortable for
fashion or men, tight jeans or tight shoes, when I
think comfort is sexy. When you're comfortable
you're free to move your body. Even Vera Wang
said a woman is never sexier than when she is
comfortable in her clothes. So taking this investiga-
tive research a bit further into the world of heels,
family friend Mike says high heels accent the tush,
the ass, the curve. Heels make it stick out more.
But Jan, his wife, says no, it's about accenting the
legs, beautifying the calf. But Mike says, "No, No,
No, that's not true," and I do think he's an expert,
but maybe he's the expert because he speaks
louder. But what the heel really does is elevate you,
quite literally, which means you can get a good
bird's eye view, or look down on someone. I know
a lot of women think heels are feminine – and they
are in a way, but they can also kill you. You can trip
and fall, twist your ankle, and be completely dis-
connected from the earth and her people and her
ways by being so far up in the high-rise of shoes.

In my world, the foot is pristine. Put a bracelet on
her and dance! Paint her up and party. Walk her
around the earth and feel the cool dust of land
under your feet. Oh, and the greatest disservice
to feet? Is concrete. Even with shoes, after twenty

blocks in New York City, your calves start to hurt. So when I arrived in India I learned there were a lot of people without shoes. And in Nepal, men trekked over mountains, rocks and stones, carrying our bags and sometimes us without shoes! And their feet were worn and old and wrinkled and parched, heavenly bits of a life, in service to those of us who came to walk their land. And I wondered what they thought of us who tour and see and take and buy and waste and exploit. Then in one village there was this little man with no feet at all. I don't know if he was born that way or if he became that way. He crawled and walked on stumps and with his hands he served me black sugary tea with such simple dignity, and his eyes twinkled. And I realized no one is looking down on us, they're just so excited and happy to have us there.

And I now know when we walk on faraway soil or maybe even in our own backyard, that we plant seeds with our step. Like planting a spirit seed back into the land, which in a future time will grow to serve some great cause. But I don't know the mechanics; it's just what I think, that we drop seeds as we travel. Like when I go to Tibet, I'll plant seeds as I walk and one day because of this, because of all the millions of seeds all the travelers have planted over there, the Tibetans will return and the Chinese will be happy about it – not because they're forced to be happy but because they'll really be happy.

You know in some traditions you're not supposed to point your feet towards a holy person and yet you can bow and touch your head to their feet? Then in other traditions, after a person dies, you're suppose to burn their shoes, destroy them so that another cannot walk in them or steal their life or be haunted by their ghost. The things we make of feet and shoes. So when I was overseas I had this thought that maybe I could bring all my shoes over that I don't wear. You see I'm not dead; I'm alive, so it would be okay. And I'd bring the ones that were in the back of the closet, so that some person, young or old, could keep their feet warm and caressed and cared for when the temperatures drop or if they start having too much concrete. So now I leave shoes in the places I go.

Ma chaussures, zapatos, sko, schuhe, scarpe, sapatos, schoenen, obuv, paduukah, paduke, kutsu, watashi no kutsu ... *(she names the word for shoes in many different languages as she lines up the pairs together.)*

Holy foot, the shoe is your temple, vessel for your holy life. *(She slowly puts on a pair of shoes and then turns to the rest of them picking up one shoe at a time.)* This was the home for my father's big feet when he walked from Israel to Turkey. *(She pauses and considers.)* Oh, there's the Mediterranean Sea there, right? Well, he walked on water! This was the home for a goat shepherd in Greece, and this was the home for the mother of a son lost in war. This was the vessel for a girl in Dachau, and these my grandmother wore. A man left these by the ocean before he walked off into the sea, and these are party shoes found next to ruins of a building that had been bombed. I imagine them dancing that night on the roof. Under the happy stars and the protective glance of a full moon. *(She dances and sings with the shoes in her arms.)*

Holy foot, the shoe is your temple, vessel for your holy life. And the seeds planted, when we walk, are not only for the earth. But the earth then, all shaking and quaking with seeds, touches the person who is bending down somewhere right now picking up a handful of dirt, or tying their sneakers or washing their feet.

This field of seeds out there holds the remnants of people, their shoes and feet. And whether we've met each other or not doesn't matter because we've walked the same land, if not in each other's shoes, so in some sense we are united. Foot to earth, earth to foot, we reach beyond this *(she indicates her flesh)* to touch heart-to-heart, soul-to-soul, and sole-to-sole.

(She leaves the shoes resting alone on the stage. Spotlight on the shoes, stage goes to black.)

Fact mixes with fancy. A dash of play dips in with a splash of fun, a slightly wacky sense of "voice," and voila, character, circumstance and story are born.

You have life experiences right now offering themselves up to you for transformation into creative streams. Use them, enjoy them, change and rearrange, and create something entirely new no one has seen or heard before.

There is a vitality, a life force, an energy, a quickening that is translated through you into action. And because there is only one you in all time, this expression is unique. And if you block it, it will never exist through any other medium … the world will not have it. It is not your business to determine how good it is, nor how valuable, nor how it compares with other expressions. It is your business to keep it yours clearly and directly, to keep the channel open.

—Martha Graham, from "Dance to the Piper."

Writing the third person

Writing third person with *he said* and *she said* is another delicious tool if you want to write about a subject matter you are too close to and need some distance from. When you want to conceal yourself or another in a story, poem, or song without revealing identity, use it. It is also a superb way to begin writing fiction when you are inspired by a true incident or a single fact. If you experiment with writing in the third-person, watch out – you may find yourself in the middle of a story.

Stretching the imagination

Imagination is an access point into your creativity. It helps you to make discoveries through imaging, dreaming, and using your genius abilities. Play with breaking up the word imagination and you can come up with I am a genie. You are the genesis, the beginning and creator through the power of imagery and imagination that uses all your senses to create: your visual apparatus, your hearing sense, tasting, touching, smelling, kinesthetic-feeling sense, and your knowing and sixth sense.

"There is no use trying," said Alice; "one can't believe impossible things."

"I dare say you haven't had much practice," said the Queen. "When I was your age, I always did it for half an hour a day. Why, sometimes I've believed as many as six impossible things before breakfast."

—Lewis Carroll

Practice: Jumping into fantasy

Dreaming up your character and walking him or her around can begin with a single fact. Put the fact in a bowl and bake with wondrous characters, bizarre plots, and intriguing themes that open, touch, and delight the taste buds in a different way than by recording what actually happened. With one piece of information your imagination can paint an entire canvas, score a musical, or write your character from freedom to prison to a paradise island to other worlds and back again. A simple recipe to enter the state of dreamer follows.

Recipe I

1. Take a single fact

» A snippet of conversation
» A line from a poem
» The remembrance of a painting seen
» A melody you can't get out of your head
» A news event from the day you were born

2. Pick a theme

» Love
» War
» Destiny
» Heroics

3. Set them in a place

» In the future, warp time, or create new worlds.
» Three thousand years in the future, in
a new climate or time zone.

4. Create new ways of doing what we routinely do today

» Washing, brushing your teeth, cooking, driving

Combine these elements to write your story of what happens and *voila*, you may have science fiction or a fantasy on your hands.

Recipe II

1. Choose a compelling fact

It can be something that helped shape the person you are. It can be as seemingly mundane as your name or where you grew up. It can be a fact of substance about anything at all in this world, or about another person or rocket science.

2. Choose an event after which you were not the same person

It can be something that happened, a marriage, birth or death. Or it can be a significant revelation you received or an insight into the nature of life.

3. Choose a profession or livelihood or none at all

4. Choose a gender, a name, an age

5. Pick a year, location and time zone

6. Write down an event that affected a large number of people

It can be something like a war, when we landed on the moon, building the Great Wall of China, a presidential election or earthquake, the Dodgers winning the World Series.

7. Write down an everyday occurrence, or even a conversation you heard or had in your life

From that everyday occurrence, the snippet of conversation, or from the large life event, begin writing through the eyes of your character incorporating the pieces of information you just wrote down. You don't have to use all the information. Pick and choose what feels right to you and for the story as it is being created. See what else springs from your imagination that you can use as source material. See if any other characters come into your play, story or song. It can even be a monologue: one person talking about an incident, a life event, their feelings or their toes. Let it rip and soar and write nonstop until you feel you are done. And have fun!!!

Travel

I always keep journals when I travel. From the journals spring monologues, which are later expanded. Fact mixes with fiction. I change and rearrange time and place. I create composites from the people I've met. Expansion occurs until something greater and more universal is discovered, explored and transmitted.

One weekend while visiting friends at their beach house, I watched their children play. When I returned to the city I was walking down the street carrying bags of groceries when words started to tumble forth. I tore off bits of the paper bag and began scribbling right there on the street. Sometimes the muse strikes at odd times. The following are the original words to the first two stanzas of a poem that later found their way into the book, *Women Celebrate: The Gift in Every Moment*.

> **Children hear a vision that sounds like the orange sun.**
> **Children see a rhythm like the beat of an ancient drum.**
> **Children in creation, stir in Mother's womb,**
> **Children of our children, Earth is where you bloom.**
>
> **From a tight little ball, you uncurl and fall into the lap**
> **Of Creation time and time again.**
> **And are hurled onto a spiraled path,**
> **One that never ends.**

Someone once asked me if I was aware that I had written, "children *see a rhythm*," and "children *hear a vision*." I think they thought I should have changed it, but it was synesthesia in action. True synesthesia is an involuntary phenomenon where people *hear colors* and *see music* and *taste sound* or where *numbers are seen as colors*. However you can intentionally invoke cross-sensory metaphors for your creative works by mixing up the senses in this most unusual and engaging way.

Experiment: Running errands

When you go out to run a chore at the store, observe everything, then come home and write it all down, everything you remember. Describe what you see, hear, touch, taste and smell – without interpretation. Then add in interpretation, meaning and reflection.

You have, right now, all the raw material from your life for story. You can travel far and wide by being a writer even if you don't leave a three-block radius or your home. Your vehicle is your imagination. Wherever you do travel, whether it is around the corner or across the sea, I encourage you to take paper and pen and scrawl down your impressions and insights. It is fascinating to read back over and it can provide material for what you will create in the future. A trip to your local grocery store or farmer's market can be a journey of many miles.

We mistake details for being picayune or only for writing about ants and bobby pins. We think of detail as small, not the realm of the cosmic mind or these big hills of NM. That isn't true. No matter how large a thing is, how fantastic, it is also ordinary. We think of details as daily and mundane. Even miracles are mundane happenings that an awakened mind can see in a fantastic way.

—Natalie Goldberg

Dreams

Dreams are wonderful places to find source material. I have a friend who literally receives dialogue for her characters in dreams. Watch and record *your* dreams for they will whisper inspirations to you in the night.

Practice

Keep a pen and paper or a tape recorder by your bed. Give yourself the suggestion that you will remember your dreams in the morning. When you wake up write down what you remember. Don't even get out of bed, just roll over and get the pen. Write down any associations you have with the dream.

If you remember nothing, then record the details of the room you are in. Then write down what you are thinking and feeling as you wake.

Take a snippet from your dream or the remembrance of a thought or feeling from when you woke, and compose a vignette, a poem or story. It can be short, even a few lines to get the tide moving. Or use your dream images to cluster with, and then write a vignette. *(See Appendix I on clustering.)*

For behind all seen things lies something vaster; everything is but a path, a portal, or a window opening on something more than itself.

—Antoine de Saint-Exupery

Breath of Celebration: Creativity in the Heart Meditation[*]

Wherever you are, lying down or sitting in a chair or taking a walk, let yourself become present to your breath: one big breath in and one long slow exhalation all the way to the bottom of your breath.

Breathe in a breath of celebration and then breathe out, softening and relaxing, releasing all the way to the bottom of your breath.

If you're somewhere where you can close your eyes, gently let your eyes close and begin to soften the face. Let the mask of the face roll back as you soften the eyes and the space between your eyes. Soften your jaw, and soften even the tongue and the teeth in your mouth.

Let a wave of softness move through your throat and come into your heart. Breathe in a wave of softness for your heart and then for your belly, let your shoulders relax down. Feel your whole body melt and soften into the seat or couch you're sitting or lying on. Whole body soft, breathing in a long, slow, deep inhalation, and a breath of celebration. Whole body happy for breath, and then exhale, letting all thoughts, past and future, release and melt away.

Slowly bring your awareness to your hands, to your fingertips. Feel the texture of your fingertips and hands. Notice the temperature. Notice if you feel sensation, like an inner hand, energy within the fingertips and hands, around your hands. Breathe and observe and notice your hands. And then let your hands and the thought of hands melt, soften, and dissolve. Breathe again into the heart and breathe out of the heart.

Bring your awareness to your feet and notice your feet, the temperature

---

* To download a free audio for this meditation, go to: www.elizabethwelles.com

of your feet and the texture of your feet, whether there is space for your feet, or whether they feel cramped. Just notice feet, if they're lying on a surface, if they're in the air. Notice your connection to foot and feet and then let that thought of feet and foot dissolve.

Bring your awareness to your heart. Breathe into your heart. Breathe into your heart and out your heart, as if you are breathing in a funnel of light, a wave of light into your heart. Then slowly let your heart center expand and widen around you. And as your heart grows out around you, so does your breath. You are now floating inside your own breath, inside your own heart, pulsing and alive, breathing in and out.

You have infinite creative wealth. It is yours. It is your gift. Whatever you are working on in your life, whatever creative endeavor you are involved with, drop that into the heart. Let it just float and melt while you rest. And let the heart's wisdom watch over your creativity.

Breathe in and breathe out. Have a sense of breathing into the heart, and bathing in beauty. Breathe beauty into every cell, fiber, and pore of your being. Breathe peace into every cell, fiber, and pore of your being. Breathe peace in and breathe peace out through yourself into the world.

Take a breath of joy, lightness, laughter, and take a breath of joy. Let this move through your whole body and as you exhale soften even more. And then breathe in energy and vitality. Breathe right into the heart through your whole body, with your whole being, breathe through every pore. And then soften more deeply into this sphere of the heart, this sphere of creativity.

In your heart lives all the formed and unformed creative wealth that has ever been and will ever be: a sphere of fluid creative ideas, wisdom, and knowledge. Breathe in and out. Soften your eyes and soften your body, breathing peace into your heart. Let your creative designs, endeavors and dreams float and be nurtured by the heart, by your breath, by the seed of celebration.

Breathe and exhale all the way to the bottom of your breath. Allow the circle of your heart that lives around you to slowly merge back through your body, melting back into the heart center. Know that the expanded heart lives and is always and ever available to you.

Take a deep breath in and out, feeling your fingertips, your hands, feeling yourself wherever you are in space, lying or sitting. Slowly and gently bring your awareness back to the body. Extending your exhalation, become aware of the sounds around you.

Know that peace is your very nature and so is creativity. May the blessings of peace and creative wisdom and health and wealth be upon you.

When you are ready, open your eyes and slowly return to your day. May it be peaceful, may it be happy, may you see beauty, may it be light.

You and the World

What must you say?

> "To write in order to change the world knowing perfectly well
> that you probably can't but also knowing that literature is
> indispensable to the world. The world changes according to the
> way people see it, and if you alter, even by a millimeter, the way
> people look at reality, then you can change it."

—James Baldwin.

There are times when what must come out of me and from me cannot
be stopped. Sometimes I wish I could stop it but there are times when
social action, justice, whatever you call it, is ignited on fire and must
be given form. It is as if there is no choice. The fire is giving birth to
something inside to save my own life that also impacts others.

What must you say? What must you say and speak or write or create
that you cannot live without saying? This chapter is about the power
of your words as social action, and the power of those words to call
forth peace. It is about no more, as in no more children off to war.
This is what I cannot, not say.

Indeed, artists – poets, novelists, and playwrights as well as musicians, painters, and actors – have shown a special aversion to war. Perhaps because, as the playwright Arthur Miller once said, "When the guns boom the arts die." But that would make their interest too self-centered; they have always been sensitive to the fate of the larger society round them. They have questioned war, whether in the fifth century before Christ, with the plays of Euripedes, or in modern times, with the paintings of Goya and Picasso.

—From *"On War"* by Howard Zinn

Words are powerful. Writers, poets, novelists, and journalists have been banished from their homelands for using them. They have had prices on their heads and they have been put to death. Books have been burned and films have been banned. Words have brought war and words have brought peace. When wielded effectively, the pen is a sword that cuts through the sham. Words have capacity to evoke, invoke, change, quake, shake and wake things up that might otherwise have remained status quo. There's not only power in words, there's great beauty, as well, in your ability to use words with wisdom, to be received by not only others, but also yourself.

What must you give voice to?

There will come a day when men will fight as children with wood swords, and they will do combat as play, and make a mockery of it.

—King Arthur.

After 9/11 I couldn't stop writing. I cried and wrote for three weeks straight. I remember a family member suggesting I try to compartmentalize my feelings. But that was not for me at that time. I felt it was part of my job to witness with the deepest part of my being what was going on in the world and in myself. That witnessing changed something in me forever. Within a year after 9/11, I received the following email in my inbox.

"SUBJECT: REMEMBER the MUSLIMS

REMEMBER the MUSLIM bombing
of Pan Am Flight 103!

REMEMBER the MUSLIM bombing of
the World Trade Center in 1993!

REMEMBER the MUSLIM bombing of
the Marine barracks in Lebanon!

REMEMBER the MUSLIM bombing of
the military barracks in Saudi Arabia!

REMEMBER the MUSLIM bombing of the
American Embassies in Africa! REMEM-
BER the MUSLIM bombing of the USS COLE!
REMEMBER the MUSLIM attack on the
Twin Towers on 9/11/2001!   9/11/2001!

REMEMBER all the AMERICAN lives that
were lost in those vicious MUSLIM attacks!

Now the United States Postal Service REMEMBERS
and HONORS, the MUSLIM holiday season with a
commemorative first class holiday postage stamp.

REMEMBER to adamantly and vocally
BOYCOTT this stamp when purchasing
your stamps at the post office.

To use this stamp would be a slap in the face
to all those AMERICANS who died at the
hands of those whom this stamp honors."

I'm a fairly levelheaded person. I don't go looking for battles, but when I read this email I started to shake and couldn't sleep. There are times when we are compelled to act, to write, to speak, as if we will burst if we don't. This was one of those times. I took the pen and composed a letter back. I worried briefly that I would offend and so took precaution in my words to try to express what needed to be said without making the woman who sent me the email seem wrong. And then I remembered a wise mentor who congratulated me after I received two attacking letters in response to my work, my words, and life. She said, "Good, now you know you're doing good work in the world." This gave me courage to send it.

What follows is the response I wrote some years ago.

> **Dear T,**
>
> **I have been thinking carefully about the email you forwarded that expressed a concern and that asked people to protest the Muslim stamps being issued. The email said over and over again,**
>
> **"Remember the Muslim bombing...
> Remember the Muslim bombing."**
>
> **At the risk of offending your political views, which I do not mean to do, I felt compelled to respond.**
>
> **People the world over are upset and fearful for all the terrorist activity that has been going on and I honor their fears. However to condemn entire populations, in this case Muslims, for the atrocities that fanatical individuals and groups commit is to only increase the polarization and violence already in existence. To condemn All Muslims for what fanatical individuals and sects do would be like condemning All Christians for the Oklahoma City bombing, the bombings of planned parent-**

hood clinics, the Salem witch trials, and the Crusades to mention a few. To condemn All Muslims would be like condemning All Americans for the Mi Lia massacre in Vietnam – and countless other massacres throughout history: the slaughter of Native American populations, African American populations, and for all the countless innocents who have been slaughtered on death row, to mention a few. To condemn All Muslims is to condemn All Chinese for the slaughter of Tibetans.

If we are to condemn entire populations: Christian, Jews, Arabs, Hindus, Seiks, Tutis, Bosnians, Croatians, Americans, Italians, French ... for what fanatical groups, parts of populations, or governments do in the name of "God" or in defense of what they think is only "their land," then we perpetrate the cycle. I pray for the end of the condemnation of entire populations, races and religions, for what a few individuals and groups take upon themselves to do.

I was born in New York and am, therefore, an American citizen, but first and foremost I am a citizen of the World. Patriotism has to extend beyond our borders to include not only America, but also the entire world, yeah the Universe. Patriotism is not, "We, Americans, are the world," but rather, the world is us, you are me and I am you, and we are the same: brothers, mothers, sisters, fathers, friends, family. That for me is what true patriotism would be, a great loving family with arms extended, our borders open, and hearts wide, able to hold the beauty and the horror, the joy and agony, the laughter, blood and tears.

We can bring peace to this planet by being peace
and that begins with ourselves. When we stop
the fighting within our hearts, when we stop the
name calling and the condemnation of others
different from our selves, then we will be able to
reach with a peaceful hand across borders to our
neighbors, our friends, even our perceived ene-
mies who have committed no harm, but through
our ignorance we fear. When we cross the barriers of fear and superstition within ourselves,
then peace in this world will have a chance.

With Blessings and In Peace,

Elizabeth

The recipient of my email didn't write an angry letter back. She didn't
even take me off her email list. Maybe it made an impact. I never found
out. But between my receiving her email and my written response,
something changed in me. I can't articulate exactly what changed or
how it changed. All I know is that I was given the opportunity to give
voice and to be a witness for love and compassion and devotion for
the world's people and in my own heart – and that counts.

We are the music makers,
And we are the dreamer of dreams,
Wandering by lone sea-breakers,
And sitting by desolate streams;
World-losers and world-forsakers,
On whom the pale moon gleams:
Yet we are the movers and shakers
Of the world for ever, it seems.

—Arthur William Edgar O'Shaughnessy

When troops were sent off to war a painter friend couldn't help but paint her sorrows through a larger than life-size canvas of Christ on the cross to depict the sorrows of those who would die in battle. That is what she had to express, that is what she had to say.

Practice: What must you give voice to?

Saying no

Describe a time in your life when you said *no* to something that meant you said *yes* to yourself. It can be as simple as saying no to a dinner date so you could have some quiet time alone. Write.

Needs that touch you

Make a list of all the places in the world where you see a need that touches you heart and soul. Write.

Compelled to speak, write, or act

Describe a time when you felt compelled to speak, write, or act on behalf of something you believed in. Write.

The news

When have you been so affected by something in the news that you couldn't sleep or cried your relief? Write.

Your service

What are the gifts of service that you bring to this world? And remember even your smile, warms words, and gentle eyes can be a gift to a world in need. Write.

Your joy

Where does your joy meet your service, meet what you are compelled to create? Write.

> *Our deepest desire is to share our riches, and this desire is rooted in the dynamics of the cosmos. What began as an outward expansion of the universe in the fireball ripens into your desire to flood all things with goodness. Whenever you are filled with a desire to fling your gifts into the world, you have become this cosmic dynamic of celebration, feeling its urgency to pour forth just as the stars felt the same urgency to pour themselves out.*

—Thomas Berry

When world events meet your muse

World events, a news story I followed, converged with my own life experience and a dream in the following poem. Again, I had to write.

24 Hours

**Yesterday morning a friend said,
"Just relax and enjoy." I said, "It's hard."**

**24 hours later I felt the amazing
blazing grace of God
and from no effort from me it came and it comes.
This blessing and miracle
happened when I was lying in bed
and suddenly Laura Ling came to my head,
one of two journalists who'd been imprisoned
in North Korea.**

**There was a circle of light around her
then around me
it is still around her and around me**

I knew this light held peace, blessing, relief,
the return of the Beloved.
I knew in this light everything was all right
and all the small focus
all disappointments washed away
no fear, no despair.

Then came a dream of purchasing paper,
a board and color
different colors I was learning about
putting them down a bit at a time
a light sky blue, a silver pearly blue
then a dark inky blue.
There was someone there as if directing or teaching
I already had some paper, and she said
in the dark blue pen it would be good to paint Ganesh
remover of obstacles, and then I awoke.

Laura and Euna, the journalists,
were in prison for four months
but you do not have to be in a prison to be in prison.
I was there, too,
imprisoned by what I embraced
and accepted as my disappointments
that I was disappointed
that I was disappointed in me
disappointed in my life

it sounds almost comical now
the belief that disappointment could ever take hold

I prayed for peace
I prayed to be content
I pray to be content with my life.

Then at the library yesterday
when I read about the girls being freed
tears welled in these eyes
but how could I cry out my relief
in the middle of books

and now the dream, strange and wondrous,
tells me a circle of light lives
nothing can take this away
it lives around you, too.

And I call on it, this light, with a dark blue pen
and with Ganesh as friend.
I turn on the TV
there are the two girls walking off the plane,
Euna bows, Laura's fists, in triumph, are raised
they have made it home again
tears race from each corner of my eyes,
nothing to catch, slow or stop them.

The blessing?
I am free
I walk the green paths
witness the death of a beloved dog
am able to dive
and bring up pearls of disappointment
and let them go
they had to come up and be freed.

Laura and Euna, you never sat in prison alone
and I now know, neither did I

welcome home, Laura and Euna
welcome home, this amazing blazing
blessing of Light.

Welcome home, Heart of my Soul.

Observe how the world affects you. Maybe a whole lot, maybe not at all. See what calls to you to write or create? What vision or dream must you convey? How do you integrate world events with your own experience? How do they impact or not impact your drive to create? What must you give voice to? What must you say? Let your muse show you the way.

More than machinery, we need humanity; more than cleverness, we need kindness and gentleness… We want to live by each other's happiness – not by each other's misery. We don't want to hate and despise one another. In this world, there is room for everyone. And the good earth is rich and can provide for everyone. The way of life can be free and beautiful.

—Charlie Chaplin

Creative Body-Politic

History on this planet includes the fact that women's bodies, men's bodies, children's bodies, and Earth's body have been battlegrounds for war. Witness the Earth though, She, who reclaims the land after being ravaged, She, who re-grows and then continues to grow after fire or flood, She, who, returns and then returns again. If Earth has this capacity for renewal, imagine our own. If our bodies hold such power that they are battleground for war, imagine how much more power they hold to be keys and ally for peace. Imagine. There is power in the body.

In the famed play, *Lysistrata*, written by Aristophanes in the fifth century B.C., the women of Athens seize control of the Acropolis, the city's treasury, *and* they refuse to have sex with their husbands who have gone to war until they make peace with Sparta. Yes, there is power in women's bodies.

A group of women once barred themselves inside a building. The men of their village were going to meet in this building to plan for war. The women didn't want war and so vowed to stay in the building until their demands were met. Additionally, the women threatened to disrobe if the men came near. To see a naked woman in this country would bring shame and disgrace to the men. So the men stayed away, the women's demands were met and peace was made.

Yes, there is power in women's bodies.

Rosa Parks stood her ground by staying seated on a bus when she was too tired to get up. Her firm stance to sit launched the civil right's movement. There is power in the body.

Martin Luther King Jr. led the civil rights movement by marching and walking and speaking and preaching. Gandhi walked and conducted hunger strikes to gain India's independence. There is power in the body.

There is power to enlighten, to mediate and rejuvenate, to heal and deepen, to suture an abyss, and uplift one's self and community. Power to reach out and touch someone with your smile, a hug and your warm hand on their shoulder. There is power through the body of your good thoughts and prayers, your listening ear, the body of your wisdom and compassion to enhance peace, creativity and joy.

A Norwegian proverb states, *"There is a Queen in every woman. Speak to the Queen and the Queen will answer."* I'd wager to say there is a Goddess in every woman, a God in every man. From the book, *Women Celebrate*:

"Such Self-recognition is the gift. For we are the salt of the earth and the givers of life, whether we make babies, food, art, whether we run businesses or corporate America. We receive seed and we then give forth. We fold in and then burst in bloom. We create and we destroy. What a capacity we have to reclaim and own the beauty, strength and compassion that is naturally ours, and that we have come here, in the flesh, to celebrate. Our hearts may be bleeding and open, but they are not broken nor will not be trampled on the ground. The Human Heart, the largest container in the Universe, is a well without end able to hold all suffering and grief, beauty, laughter, and relief. We are strong in our vulnerabilities, unshakable in our collective resolve, and this landscape for celebration and honor of life is available not only to women, but to all people everywhere, right now. It is a landscape to be embraced as real in our hearts, for it already is."

Questions for your body of power

Stop and feel your body in space.

» Scan your body and ask where does the power lie?
» Describe your body and its power.
» What about your body is powerful?
» What about your body is beautiful?
» What kind of signals does your body give you?
» What do you know about your body as ally?
» Describe a time when you knew power *through* your body.
» How does it express itself, this, your body of power?
» What happens when it is suppressed?
» What happens when it is released?

Are you a painter with the gift of eyes to see exquisite color and transfer that onto the canvas with your hands, a dancer with the ability to fly in the sky? Are you an architect with the gift to build visions others can see? Are you a lawyer with the gift of speech? Are you a nurse with hands that heal? A writer who feels? A scientist who explores the brain?

» Describe how you channel the power of your body.
» Towards what purpose, vision, goal or dream?

We live in a world where power is measured by doing. What if you did nothing to experience power?

» What do you know about your body as ally for peace?
» Can you feel, envision or know the body
  of peace in your body now?

Imagine a world where you live with your powerful Self, your powerful body, your body of peace, and the world at peace.

» Describe this world, the earth, your body and Self.
» Describe how your life would look.
» Describe your unique stream of creativity in this world.
» Where do you live and how is your life different?

I have and still am a seeker,
but I have ceased to question stars and books;
I have begun to listen to the teaching my blood whispers to me.

—Hermann Hesse

Your Body of Power, Body of Peace Meditation

Soften and melt any ideas that you have about your body, about power and about peace. In your imagination find yourself before a fire outside under the stars. And strip away any clothes you have on, any conditions, any old thoughts or feelings that have held you back or paralyzed you in any way. Throw into the fire any fears or trepidations, throw into the fire the old past and everything that has held you back from your powerful self. Toss into the fire anything that has kept you from your creativity and peace. Throw it all into the fire and let the flames melt what no longer belongs in your life.

Take a deep breath and relax. Take another deep breath and soften your mouth and eyes as you exhale. Relax your shoulders. Relax your heart and the area around your throat and neck. Relax your belly, your hips, your arms and legs, your hands and feet. Relax and feel yourself fresh born. Know yourself fresh new born. There is strength in this knowing, a knowing that anything is possible. Feel the strength of this knowing as you begin to build a new body of creativity, power and peace.

Imagine you can dress in anything you want. And begin to assemble this wardrobe by first finding your cloth of creativity. Be as wild or earthy or practical as you desire. Maybe you find yourself dressing in a rainbow of feathers, maybe you are wrapped in paint, you as canvas, maybe you are clothed in silks or robes, a specter of light or garments of gold. Find yourself in your garment of creativity. Be in your garment of creativity. Breathe in long, slow, and deep from your own creative core, your own talents, your strengths, and your gifts. Breathe in your creative self. Breathe in and relax.

Now find or choose, or let come to you, the cloth for your body of power. What colors and textures are woven into your garment of power? What would your body look like if it were clothed in power? How would your body feel clothed in power? What song would your body of power sing? What kind of dance would it do? And what does power mean to you? Confidence? Strength? The ability to move or the ability to be still in a storm? Power. Maybe you are clothed by the weather Gods: by wind or the rains or the Great Celestial Sun or by the galaxies and stars. Maybe it is a simple dress or a suit of armor, talons or wings you grow and wear. What does power mean to you? Power to act? Protection? Silence? Peace and creative well-being? Power. Know and feel power within your own self, body, heart, mind and soul. Breathe in yourself as knowing and power-filled. Breathe through every fiber, pore and cell of your being. Breathe in through your feet, your hands, your heart, your belly and your head. Breathe.

Breathe and relax.

Bathe your body in the light of the fire, in the light of illumination. Bathe yourself with peace rays from the light of the moon or the sun or the sky. Breathe in peace and breathe out peace, whatever this means to you. Clothe yourself in your body of peace. Feel and know peace in and through every pore, fiber, and cell of your being. Peace.

Breathe and stand and bathe yourself in the light of peace and let this peace become the cloth you wear and the cloth you weave. Peace as your outer garment and inner garment, peace as the foundation upon which your creativity and power rest.

Stand before the fire. Whether you see it or not, it is here. Whether there is proof or not, it is here. Your imagining power, the power of your creativity and of your knowing is here now. Simply breathe and trust in this. Trust in your own peace, in your power, in your creativity. Breathe in luminous radiant light, illuminating your well-being.

Breathe in and relax and feel yourself whole, inside your body and outside around your body.

Breathe and relax and rest in your Self.

Creativity Feeds Creativity

As a child and young adult, complete tunes and words poured through my head when walking outside. By the time I got home they were gone. The muse strikes at odd hours and you have to be prepared to meet her, best you can. Now I am. Paper sits by my bed, and usually there are pens and paper in the car and often on my person. When driving cross-country, a tape recorder sits on the passenger seat. If I am on an especially creative swing, I may take pen and paper to scrawl on as I watch the opening credits of a film, for sometimes activities overlap, words still swirling from a project left behind at home. Not all the words find their way into anything of import. In fact, most of them are left on the cutting room floor.

Sometimes creative embers find resonance and activation through a group of people or another individual. Music industry professionals often spurred my creative fires when they'd say of my work, "Oh, great line, can I use that?" Singing, music, songwriting have always held a special place in my life. And so finally I attended a songwriter's group to investigate this form of playing with the word. People came to create, nurture and hone their skills. Seasoned songwriters, more adept at this skill than I, patiently heard my words and week after week kindly said, "That's a poem, not a song." One week I worked and reworked and worked again my song. By the time I finished reading it to the group, they jumped to their feet and yelled, "That's a rap song! You wrote a rap song!"

While the nature of creativity is that it is always there, I have met a few that have quietly asked, "Can you turn the creative dial down?" I laugh at that and smile knowingly. Millions hunger for more creativity, but there are some for whom the muse is awake all the time. Imagine that. The She-He muse *is* awake all the time and what those few have done is to attune themselves to Him or Her. But if you are one of the hungering masses in search for more creative outlets in your life, know that creativity feeds creativity.

Wherever you are, find the places and spaces of inspiration for you. Search them out. Put yourself around other creative people. Join a group that stirs your creative juice. Walk outside in nature, by the beach or at the mountains, in a crowded mall or through a storm. With books or paint or science or math or color and design prompt your imagination to greater wakefulness. Explore and learn something new. Dare to grow in the direction of what you love, in the direction of what gives you energy, in the direction of your dreams. The embers of your creativity, glowing active and alive, are always there and only wait for you to turn towards them.

Below is the rap song composed in 2001. It was a strong rap that stretched from war to peace.

The Holy That Is Shunned, Part I

Verse 1

He was a man of the street, who'd seen better days,
When he made a decent living and got a yearly raise,
He fought hard for himself when he was feeling down,
Carving poems in snow on the ground.
He read the headlines of war, just words on a page,
But in his heart they took center stage
Simple tears across his face, tremors in the human race

Verse 2

Old men hauled up on a broken down bench
Chugging cheap wine, breathing the stench
Finding shelter under cardboard in the rain
They fall dead asleep on a heaven-bound train.
Witnesses to the tremors, contestants in a race
Their lives a book, closed without trace.

Chorus

The Holy that is shunned,
They are the forgotten ones
They witness devastation,
And the world's procrastination
The Holy that is shunned,
They are the forgotten ones

Verse 3

Mothers and daughters hold in their arms
The old and the dying, the young and forlorn,
Whose earthly ties dim as they hear whispered hymns,
And the Blessed see clearly through salt-stung eyes,
Their tears scour earth, for their hearts are wise

To cry for the dying, who are deplored
They are the Silent witnesses, knocking at the door.

Chorus

The Holy that is shunned,
They are the forgotten ones
They witness devastation
And the world's procrastination
The Holy that is shunned,
They are the forgotten ones.

(Musical interlude)

The Holy That Is Shunned, Part II

Verse 1

She's a woman of the land, just like you or me,
With simple dreams of life, for her child to be free
She lived with a cloth that veiled her head,
Words shut up in her heart, until she fled
But her captors wanted blood,
Her body was found left out in the mud
Spirits watch helpless, their potency erased
Tears slip from their eyes, tremors in the human race

Verse 2

Shape-shifting sister appearing like steam
Lonesome nameless brother haunting my dreams
Howl of sons, tortured out in the cold,
Cries from daughters, raped on dusty roads,
Witnesses to the tremors, contestants in a race

Their lives a book, closed without trace.
Blood on the land, messengers at hand,

Bridge

They don't live lives considered noble by most
But they are the world's Holiest Ghosts
Hungering in the streets of war-ravaged lands
Eating up the homeless, woman, child and man.
They are the holy ones
Vanishing without a trace
They are the Holy ones
Their lives, a testament to the human race

Chorus

The Holy that is shunned,
They are the forgotten ones
They witness devastation,
And the world's procrastination
The Holy that is shunned,
They are the forgotten ones.

Verse 3

Mothers of all nations stand in alarm
Commanding the Captains to lay down their arms
There is no choice; their voices rise higher
They carry on their songs, the world's finest choir
The Silent Witnesses, silent no more,
Are the Holy Ones raging at the door,
They are the named and the nameless,
Bringing peace to war
The named and the nameless,
Dreaming peace forevermore.

Chorus

The Holy that is shunned, and the Remembered Ones
They witness devastation, the world's procrastination

The Holy that is shunned, and the Remembered Ones
Some here and some gone, vanished without a trace,
All their lives, a testament to the human race
They are the nameless and the named,
Bringing peace to war
The nameless and the named,
Dreaming peace forevermore
Some here and some gone, vanished without a trace,
All their lives, all their lives a testament
To the human race.

Thank you to the people and groups, the nameless and the named, past, present and future, that have contributed to stirring the creative embers of my Soul. May our creative lives be a testament to peace, forevermore.

A Musing on Doubt, Belief, Knowing and Peace

In the privacy of thought I have sometimes questioned if this earth will ever be without war. The idealist I am hesitates to write that, but my inner skeptic has wondered, why, with powerful and creative peace efforts, long in history, does it seem we are not further along in enduring peace? But then beauty whisks me away to what I know, see, and experience directly. Tiny buds perched on a thawing branch of snow, the curl of baby fingers, each tiny nail a perfection, orphaned children in lands with little to eat and nowhere to sleep but still hungry for learning and school. How could I ever doubt for what is yet to come for this great earth?

But then I smile, remembering a teacher who once said to the class, "That which you doubt is where you must go. It is proof of your belief, belief in yourself, your creative passions, your vision and voice." If you doubt yourself then you must move towards the Self. If you doubt your creativity then that is where your strength lies. If you doubt peace can be realized by this great earth, then move in that direction of peace for Her and its people.

This is a revolution in thought. Considering that most of us would prefer less doubt concerning our chosen ideals, it was an enlightening view. If we view doubt as an intellectual, even left-brained process here, instead of a fearful state of confusion, then we gain some clues.

Doubt has had its evolutionary advantage and value. When we were in the jungles, doubt ensured our bodily survival. Doubts that spoke to us in the privacy of our primitive thoughts, "Eh, maybe don't go into the cave of the wooly mammoth, not now, even if we are a tad chilly. We'll survive the night with just the fire, thank you." It was helpful, then. It kept us safe. But too often this ancient survival mechanism casts a shadow on our ability to take healthy risks today. Lives are left crippled or at least there is a crimp in our style. We too closely question our instincts making null and void intuitive direction for a rich and fuller life. Doubt, like an umbrella trying to shield us from the storm, is now put up on sunny days so that we don't get out to play!

But what if doubt, turned on its head, is a kind of wonder, a hopeful looking up with curiosity or courage? Would "doubt" then reflect belief and be ally to the direction I must personally travel and to what I must say? Doubts have been a part of my landscape on Earth. So now I honor them, remembering what that teacher said, looking more closely to see if, in a reverse kind of fashion, they can point the way to what I hold close to my heart.

And what does belief mean anyway? Beliefs are not something I've ever held sacrosanct. I recognize how people fight for their beliefs, pouring their hearts into what they believe they love, and then next thing you know, their belief changes as the wind. In some circles, belief is held up to be the magic bullet. Believe enough and something will come. As if we can will with our minds what will occur, changing outcome with personal desire and taste. And if desired outcome didn't arrive, then there is the converse correlation that you didn't believe enough! But that's too didactic and punishing. Because believe me, (pun intended) I've probably suffered more doubt in my life.

Although I won't make a belief God and King, beliefs can be likened to rungs on a ladder or stepping stones to higher ideals.* Belief can reflect a level of confidence offering a gift, supplying the energy and perseverance to keep on keeping on. It allows for a clear funnel between energy and action in the creative process, without excess diversion and debris getting in the way. As the scenery changes, as the temperature soars, as waves roll onto the shore, *having belief in what you already know deep in your heart makes life easier* simply because there is confidence and trust, perseverance and patience, to outlast the rockier, less steady times. Belief isn't necessary to what we know or don't know, to what comes or doesn't come into our lives. It is simply a sign along the way.

For it is a Knowing that has kept me moving along my path despite the, at times, shaky belief in myself. The Soul's Knowing, deeper than belief, a Knowing without bound, a Knowing that knows without explanation or analysis. It is the animal's Knowing it is going to rain, the Knowing of who is on the other end of the phone when you hear the first ring. It is the heart's Knowing that allows for a more fluid acceptance of the ups and down, the ebb and flow, as you ride through life.

Knowing that is not only intuitive but also garnered through experience, practical and wise. Knowing that sometimes sits you down to set out the information that lies before you; Knowing that stealthily plants in that information seeds for elevation, revelation and illumination that ensure your survival – even when you doubt.

Belief is held in the body of this Knowing. When plagued by confusion, suffering doubt, and no belief, it is my Knowing that steps in to safely keep me going with courage, strength and conviction. Even

---

* Beliefs likened to stepping-stones or ladders comes from the teachings of Inayat Khan.

when fear splatters confidence on the ground, I move my feet without knowing why, but ever-Knowing I must move as intuition instructs, like people in dark valleys feeling for light, stumbling and falling, rising and walking out and on.

But being a student of the word, I wanted to understand more deeply this word "belief," and so in my qualms I investigated its meaning, to see how I could perhaps reframe it for myself, hoping to make it more friendly and familiar than the idol and easy platitude I had seen it become. I suspected deeper roots or an ancient meaning that had been lost through time.

Godlieve is the name of a friend of mine. She is named after the saint, Godlieve. We call her Lieve. I started to wonder about the lieve in her name and about the lieve in be-lieve and re-lieve. So I searched online and also asked her what Lieve and Lief meant.

Beloved, sweet, dear were among the meanings. And so it followed that be-lief then means to be beloved and re-lief means return of the beloved. When you believe in something you are following it with your love, it is an action of the heart. When you are relieved, the beloved and feelings of sweetness return. My heart sang with that – these were meanings I could wrap my arms around!

So next time you doubt yourself or something you are passionate about, take a step back, and instead look with wonder to see if it's not your belief in disguise, and that which you love held in the body of your Knowing. If doubt can be proof of your belief, as that teacher told the class years ago, then belief is a column of support under the temple of your Knowing. And as far as I'm concerned, feeling the beloved within the Knowing strengthens and lifts me up.

We Have Our Songs

I look across time in wonder for who we are,
From where we came
To where we've come, to where we'll go
And I honor the movements
The struggles, the victories,
The nameless and the named
No longer doubting the veracity
Of what has occurred
Or that the voice of one person can echo a call
Through the cells of the land,
People and their ideals.
I see the rising up of dreams,
Poetry in heart, written on tongues
Rhythm in feet, dance in the street, strong with song
And even when all appears lost
With nothing to sing for
There is the timber and timbre of Knowing
That keeps us going
To hear a creative quiet peace rocking
In the delicate branches of our lives
This Knowing that we must still sing
For what else is there if we don't have our songs.

An Open Letter from The Spirit of Peace

*If we saw ourselves with eyes of unconditional love,
the wars inside ourselves and in the world would cease.
We'd all melt into little puddles – that bounce!*

Dear Reader,

I, The Spirit of Peace, once met a man who had been a peace activist his entire life, a soldier and warrior for peace. His sudden departure from Earth was because, at the hands of violence, he took his own life. Distraught and in despair, thinking all his peace efforts had been for naught. For war still existed on our planet and this was all he could see and so he felt a failure in his heart.

In this matter, I would direct you to a quote by the great Trappist monk, Thomas Merton.

There is a pervasive form of contemporary violence to which the idealist, fighting for peace by nonviolent means, most easily succumbs; activism and overwork. The rush and pressure of modern life are a form, perhaps the most common form, of its innate violence. To allow oneself to be carried away by a multitude of conflicting concerns, to surrender to too many demands, to commit oneself to too many projects, to want to help everyone, is to succumb to violence. More than that, it is cooperation in violence. The frenzy of the activist neutralizes their work for peace. It destroys their own inner capacity for peace. It destroys the fruitfulness of their work because it kills the inner wisdom which makes their work fruitful.

Dear Reader, there will always be a greater peace inside of you than in the world because I, The Spirit of Peace, come *from you.* As social activists you may not see the connection between inner and outer peace, but it is there. Your creativity is greater than anything "out there." Your spirit is stronger than anything on this earth. And this is because peace, creativity and strength come *from you.*

Peacemakers, I gently implore and even challenge you to find peace within. It is there. It doesn't mean to stop working for peace in the world, but balance your work with play and joy, and with quiet inner contemplative activities that give you solace and rest. Be gentle with yourselves and ask how do you find peace? How do you walk with me in your life, amidst your daily activities? How do you remind yourself I, The Spirit of Peace, exist? Let not even your creativity with its joyful frenzy take you away from me, but allow it to stir me deeper into your hearts.

Your personal well-being as peacemaker – if this is the role you've chosen for yourself or that has been thrust upon you – is vital as you go about your work. This does not mean you will always be the ultimate in calm. This does not mean you will not encounter agitation and moments of anger or sorrow or grief. What it means is that your peace matters. It matters that you nurture self-care and practice kindness towards yourself as best you can. For your practice will radiate silently out, peace will spread and prevail.

If you want, look at me as the Ocean of Peace in which you live out your life, where every thing is seen, known, touched, accepted and loved. Even all the hard, messy stuff, has its body in me.

Elizabeth has a friend named Wayne. She once tried to find the words to describe him. She didn't think he described himself as a Buddhist, but wasn't sure how he described himself and so asked. "No," he said, "you're right. I don't describe myself as a Buddhist."

"What do you say of yourself when someone asks?"

"I say I'm on the path of awareness according to the teachings of Buddha."

"And what path would you say I'm on?" Elizabeth asked.

"I'd say you're on the path of love."

"And peace?"

He nodded.

"But I'm not always loving and peaceful," Elizabeth said.

"And I'm not always aware," Wayne smiled.

Such is the path. You fall off, you get back on, and you keep on keeping on. But even the "fall off" is part of the "path." From falling you gain experience. Through experience, you gain wisdom, understanding and compassion.

Dear Reader, you are the embodiments of Divine Loving Souls, know I am ever by your side. I surround you. You breathe and have your life in me. I live in you and come from you. I am forever yours.

In Loving Service,
The Spirit of Peace

Through journaling and meditation

lay your burdens down

*

Journaling and meditation support a life

of healing, creativity, joy and peace

*

Listen and hear into the space

between what was and what will be

*

Embrace mystery

*

And Celebrate

Appendix I: What's Clustering?

This is a cluster.

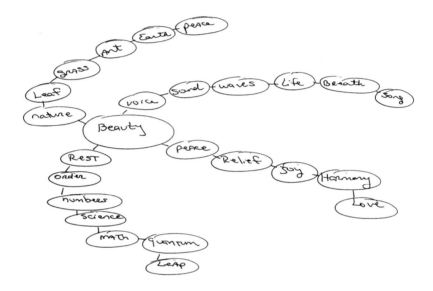

Clustering is a pre-writing tool that allows you to write naturally and freely.

It is a valuable practice and the number one book on the subject is Gabriele Lusser Rico's book, *Writing the Natural Way.* Clustering can be of assistance in everything from the free-associate spilling out of thought to writing poetry to helping you organize chapters in a book. My advice is to get the book, use it and reuse it. In lieu of that, here is a brief understanding of this valuable practice.

Clustering is a free-associative brainstorming process that allows you to pour out ideas, words and language, free from the critic, free from evaluation of any kind. The initial phase of clustering is the rush of raw material, the surge to create unbound. Words that appear random and nonlinear have the opportunity to fall onto the page until you begin to see patterns emerge.

The second part of clustering is when you recognize the patterns, the images and words that tie together. Suddenly you have a map before you and a direction for the flow of your ideas. Sometimes you can even see the entire scope of where you are going.

Clustering can be likened to the farmer looking out over his unplowed fields. All the images of land and growth are before him. In a jumble he sees trees, earth, sky, crops, crop rotation, peas, corn, horses, chickens, cows, rain, fertilizer, sun, stalks, green, and hay. The entire season and all the possibilities for what he could plant are there. Then, in a sudden moment of insight and clarity, he says to himself: Beans, melons, tomatoes, oats and corn. He knows what he wants to plant. He can see the field full, where all the crops will lay, and he can now begin to plow the pasture.

The initial phase of clustering, the unbound free associations that rush or even gush from the writer, artist, and creator, lies in one's ability to tap into the right hemisphere of the brain, or what Gabriele Lusser Rico calls the Design mind. The Design mind knows how to deal with ambiguity and paradox, novelty and the unknown. It is the part of us that is sensitive to rhythm and wholeness, the part of us that some call the 'right brain.'

Then there is another part of us that can see parts and sequence, the logical and rational. This she calls the Sign mind or the left hemisphere of the brain. Both the Design mind and the Sign mind are needed for creative endeavors. But the Sign mind naturally flows *from* the Design mind.

You begin clustering by choosing a seed word or phrase as your nucleus. Write the word or phrase in the middle of your paper and circle it. Let yourself free-associate off that word or phrase. In the above diagram the word *beauty* was chosen. Lightning images in the form of words (or even pictures, squiggles and lines) will pour forth. Spill them onto the page by drawing a line from your nucleus outward. Write the next word down and circle it. Then another word will automatically rise to your consciousness. Draw another line from the second circle outward, writing down the next word and circling that. Continue on until there is a natural conclusion. You now have one branch of your cluster.

Return to the original nucleus, word or phrase, and begin a new branch. You may have one branch, two branches or multiple branches stemming from one nucleus. Cluster until you feel complete.

Clustering is a self-organizing process. As you write down what seems like random words or phrases around the nucleus, circling those words or phrases and continuing out in a stream of branches, you will suddenly see a pattern or patterns form until you have that familiar and happy "I've got it! Yes! Aha!" feeling. It is the same joyful feeling that leads you in the direction of what gives you energy. Your focus becomes clear. You can see the road ahead. Details come into focus. You are compelled to move and you begin writing easily in the direction of your recognition.

Look at your cluster and let it speak to you. Like a map, words or groups of words will form connections. Begin writing a vignette or short poem from your cluster. You do not have to use all the words or phrases from the cluster. This is where your selective Sign mind comes in to choose, map out, and create.

It's like lying on your back on a warm summer day. Your wandering eye looks at the sky to see all the clouds floating by. The freeform Design mind sees in those clouds random associations from your lifetime of experience. The Sign mind gets involved when you suddenly see patterns in the clouds to recognize a horse, an octopus, a spaceship or cow. The initial wandering and associations is the Design mind's action. The pulling together of the elements is the Sign mind. One gift of the Design mind is that it blocks the censor of the Sign mind. While you are designing your cluster you are not thinking, "Oh this isn't working, this doesn't go there." The evaluative process is put on hold giving you the power to conjure and find the raw material first.

I have seen clients find valuable insights into their organizational process using clusters. One woman came to a journaling workshop and announced that she wasn't organized and didn't know how to organize. After she clustered, clear organization stood out on the page. Each branch of her cluster spoke to a different and specific area of her life. She learned that she was, indeed, organized. Only her organizational process did not occur in a linear fashion.

With this method I have witnessed beginning writers take the leap away from staid writing to find richer imagery, evocative insights and a new aliveness for their poetry, stories, and general language abilities. It's a great tool I cannot say enough about. I would encourage you to get Rico's book, use it, and watch your writing soar.

Appendix II: Inspirational Quotes on Creativity, Writing & Life

A writer needs three things, experience, observation, and imagination, any two of which, at times any one of which, can supply the lack of the others.

—William Faulkner

I dare not pretend to be any other than the secretary – the authors are in eternity.

—William Blake

To let each impression and each embryo of a feeling come to completion, entirely in itself, in the dark, in the unsayable, the unconscious beyond the reach of one's own understanding, and with deep humility and patience, to wait for the hour when a new clarity is born. This alone is what it means to live as an artist in understanding as in creating.

—Rainer Maria Rilke

The more you wish to describe a Universal the more minutely and truthfully you must describe a Particular.

—Brenda Ueland

*It is not because things are difficult that we do not dare;
It is because we do not dare that they are difficult.*

—Seneca

Thank goodness I was never sent to school. It would have rubbed off some of the originality.

—Beatrix Potter (1866-1943)

Until one is committed, there is hesitancy, the chance to draw back, always ineffectiveness. Concerning all acts of initiative (and creation), there is one elementary truth the ignorance of which kills countless ideas and splendid plans: that the moment one definitely commits oneself, then providence moves too. A whole stream of events issues from the decision, raising in one's favor all manner of unforeseen incidents, meetings and material assistance, which no man could have dreamt would have come his way. I learned a deep respect for one of Goethe's couplets: "Whatever you can do or dream you can, begin it. Boldness has genius, power and magic in it!"

—W. H. Murray

The aim of art is to represent not the outward appearance of things, but their inward significance.

—Aristotle

If eyes were made for seeing, then Beauty is its own excuse for being.

—Ralph Waldo Emerson

In a real sense all life is inter-related.
All persons are caught in an inescapable network of mutuality, tied in a single garment of destiny.
Whatever affects one directly affects all indirectly.
I can never be what I ought to be until you are what you ought to be, and you can never be what you ought to be until I am what I ought to be.
This is the inter-related structure of reality.

—Reverend Martin Luther King, Junior

True art lies in a reality that is felt.

—Odilon Redon

There are more things in heaven and earth than are dreamt of in your philosophies, Horatio.

—Shakespeare

Fill your paper with the breathings of your heart.

—William Wordsworth

I continue to create because writing is a labor of love and also an act of defiance, a way to light a candle in a gale wind...

—Alice Childress

And the day came when the risk to remain tight in a bud was more painful than the risk it took to blossom.

—Anais Nin

Look to this day, for it is the life, the very life of life.

—From the Sanskrit

It is art that makes life, makes interest, makes importance and I know of no substitute whatever for the force and beauty of its process.

—Henry James

Imagination is the eye of the Soul.

—Joseph Joubert

Everything that lives is holy.

—William Blake

This little light of mine, I'm gonna let it shine.

—Langston Hughes

Appendix III: Books on Writing, Inspiration & Imagination

If You Want to Write, by Brenda Ueland/Graywolf Press

Writing Down the Bones, by Natalie Goldberg/Shambhala

The Writer's Journey, by Christopher Vogler/
Michael Wiese Productions

Storytelling & The Art of Imagination,
by Nancy Mellon/Element

Finding What You Didn't Lose, by John Fox/
Jeremy P. Tarcher/Putnam Book

The Artist's Way, by Julia Cameron/
Jeremy P. Tarcher/Putnam Book

Letters to a Young Poet, by Rainer Maria Rilke/Vintage Books

Gift from the Sea, by Anne Morrow Lindbergh/
New American Library

Centering, by M.C. Richards/Wesleyan University Press

Bird by Bird, by Anne Lamott/Anchor Books/Random House

Free Play, by Stephen Nachmanovitch/
Jeremy P. Tarcher/Putnam Book

Writing the Natural Way, by Gabriele Lusser Rico/
Jeremy P. Tarcher/St. Martin's Press

*Shimmering Images: A Handy Little Guide to Writing
Memoir,* by Lisa Dale Norton/St. Martin's Press

Meet Elizabeth Welles

Elizabeth Welles is a performance artist, poet, and writer dedicated to nurturing the seeds of creativity, joy, and peace that reside in the human heart. Elizabeth especially loves the art of storytelling in any form, be it on the stage or the page.

A naturally gifted speaker, Elizabeth immediately puts her audiences at ease – whether in India, Japan, Nepal, Europe or at home in the United States – sharing and celebrating the common threads of humanity that connect us all.

Elizabeth is the editor of the book, *Women Celebrate: The Gift in Every Moment,* the creator of the CD, *Meditation for Relaxation,* and the founder of *The Four Wisdoms of Creativity*™ and *The ISIS Method for Stress Reduction.* She regularly performs her one-woman shows, *Speak the Lands of My Heart,* about a journey to India, and *Water from the Welles,* an entertaining collection of monologues, stories, poems and songs that connect the listener to their own inner resources of wisdom and compassion.

Elizabeth facilitates workshops on journaling, story, meditation and relaxation to enhance creativity, laughter, and peace.

To download your FREE meditation to enhance relaxation and creativity, and for information on Elizabeth's work, please visit: www.ElizabethWelles.com

For more information:

Peace Communications
1129 Maricopa Highway #200
Ojai, CA 93023
(323) 682-4025
info@elizabethwelles.com

CPSIA information can be obtained at www.ICGtesting.com
Printed in the USA
BVOW031114101211

278017BV00006B/1/P

9 780974 399812